THE CONTENTED SOUL

THE ART OF SAVORING LIFE

LISA GRAHAM MCMINN

IVP Books

An imprint of InterVarsity Press
Downers Grove, Illinois

InterVarsity Press
P.O. Box 1400, Downers Grove, IL 60515-1426
World Wide Web: www.ivpress.com
E-mail: mail@ivpress.com

InterVarsity Press® is the book-publishing division of InterVarsity Christian Fellowship/USA®, a student movement active on campus at hundreds of universities, colleges and schools of nursing in the United States of America, and a member movement of the International Fellowship of Evangelical Students. For information about local and regional activities, write Public Relations Dept., InterVarsity Christian Fellowship/USA, 6400 Schroeder Rd., P.O. Box 7895, Madison, WI 53707-7895, or visit the IVCF website at <www.intervarsity.org>.

Unless otherwise indicated, all Scripture quotations are taken from the Holy Bible, New Living Translation, copyright ©1996. Used by permission of Tyndale House Publishers, Inc., Wheaton, Illinois 60189. All rights reserved.

Design: Cindy Kiple
Images: Karen Beard/Getty Images

ISBN-10: 0-8308-3335-8
ISBN-13: 978-0-8308-3335-1

Printed in the United States of America ∞

Library of Congress Cataloging-in-Publication Data

McMinn, Lisa Graham, 1958-
   The contented soul: the art of savoring life/Lisa Graham McMinn.
      p. cm.
   Includes bibliographical references and index.
   ISBN-13: 978-0-8308-3335-1 (cloth: alk. paper)
   ISBN-10: 0-8308-3335-8 (cloth: alk. paper)
   1. Christian life. I. Title.
   BV4501.3.M378   2006
   248.4—dc22

                                                                      2005033147

| P | 18 | 17 | 16 | 15 | 14 | 13 | 12 | 11 | 10 | 9 | 8 | 7 | 6 | 5 | 4 | 3 | 2 |
| Y | 20 | 19 | 18 | 17 | 16 | 15 | 14 | 13 | 12 | 11 | 10 | 09 | 08 | 07 | 06 |

In memory of my father
Ward G. Graham
1934-2004

CONTENTS

ACKNOWLEDGMENTS

Many people have taught me that contentment comes from noticing small and large wonders that remind us of God's faithful love and comforting presence. I am indebted to my father, who taught me to look for silver linings in storm clouds, and instilled in his children hope and courage to try to live rightly in each moment, with integrity and virtue. My dear friends Jana and Edee pull me into unexpected adventures and keep me mindful of God's presence and the goodness and beauty that yet prevail amidst ashes. Colleagues and students at Wheaton College inspire me by their good and faithful work for justice and peace; they remind me that people are freed from the tyranny of oppressive regimes, and sometimes from the tyranny of poverty, ushering in the possibility for *shalom*—contentment rooted in what is just and good. Thank you all.

Jeff Crosby, marketing director at IVP, caught the vision for what was possible in this book and carried it through to the end. He gave me encouragement when I needed it and has been a tremendous support at every point along the way. Cindy Bunch is a wonderful and warm editor, giving me guidance as my focus for the book shifted. Ruth Goring spiffed up my sentences and corrected my grammatical mistakes. Brooke Nolen, Allison Rieck, Peter Mayer, Bob Fryling and others at IVP each contributed in getting this book from my head to your hands. The folks at IVP have been terrific to work with.

And finally, I want to thank Mark, my dear friend, husband and sojourner for twenty-seven years. He speaks truth and extends grace to me, and has taught me much about contentment.

AN INVITATION
TO CONTENTMENT

O Lord God, grant us peace, for you have given us all things. Grant us the
peace of quietness, the peace of the Sabbath which has no evening.

ST. AUGUSTINE

Chale (Shay-lee), my old Border-collie-mix, and I have run together for twelve years. We do this only about once a week now, given her aging body, and mine. On other days we walk. Autumn outings satisfy us the most. Sometimes a mist rises from the pond we pass on our way to Winfield Mounds, and as we cross the bridge over the DuPage River we occasionally spot deer feeding in the water. Chale is old enough to resist the chase; instead she perks up her ears and lifts her nose to inhale what she can of deer, squirrel and rabbit. I am old enough to release myself from the pressure to Keep Moving and can stand and watch—appreciating the wonder of sharing the world with creatures that continue to live relatively unchanged by the changing world around them.

In the fall the squirrels scour for nuts, the perennials go into hibernation, the cicadas and crickets die off, and the Canadian geese fly south. When Chale and I walk through the neighborhood, I kick through leaves the wind has blown into piles against the curb. They crunch and crackle beneath my feet. When Chale stops to mark her territory, I pick up maple, oak and ash leaves that I will press and then dip into melted wax at home and display through Thanksgiving.

At night I'll light a fire in the fireplace, and a few candles besides. The warm flames and scents of wood and wax comfort me during these shortening days and lengthening nights. Another year marked by autumn routines, sustained by the presence of God.

We are surrounded by simple pleasures and the possibility of sipping and savoring our very earthy, very physical life. Contentment awaits us, inviting us to savor each moment, and in doing so to honor the God who gave us life.

Yet most of us find contentment elusive. Although we are encouraged to pursue our dreams and aspire to great things, we are marginally content at best. Actually it all does make sense. If I have high expectations to be content and fulfilled and perceive myself as being obligated to stretch toward happiness, then I am likely to focus on what I do not possess and pursue choices that might make me more satisfied. At any point I can switch jobs, drop one significant relationship to pick up another, change churches, and relocate out of my neighborhood or community. My ability to be content will be undermined by my high expectations for happiness and fulfillment.

Too easily we live unexamined and disconnected lives, distracting ourselves in our quest for greater ease, comfort or the acquisition of better stuff. But there is another way that leads toward a more certain contentment. From a Roman prison Paul writes the church in Philippi and tells them that he has learned the secret of being content:

Always be full of joy in the Lord. I say it again—rejoice! Let everyone see that you are considerate in all you do. Remember, the Lord is coming soon.

Don't worry about anything; instead, pray about everything. Tell God what you need, and thank him for all he has done. If you do this, you will experience God's peace, which is far more wonderful than the human mind can understand. His peace will guard your hearts and minds as you live in Christ Jesus.

And now, dear brothers and sisters, let me say one more thing as I close this letter. Fix your thoughts on what is true and honorable and right. Think about things that are pure and lovely and admirable. Think about things that are excellent and worthy of praise. Keep putting into practice all you learned from me and heard from me and saw me doing, and the God of peace will be with you. . . .

For I have learned how to get along happily whether I have much or little. I know how to live on almost nothing or with everything. I have learned the secret of living in every situation, whether it is with a full stomach or empty, with plenty or little. For I can do everything with the help of Christ who gives me the strength I need. (Phil 4:4-9, 11-13)

God's goodness and Jesus' incarnation, life, death and resurrection are the source of Paul's contentment, and ours. Without this foundation our contentment risks being shallow, temporal, rooted in uncertain circumstances.

God conquered evil, liberating and reconciling the world through the atoning work of Christ. In an act of divine and supreme love, God showed that compassion is greater than the world's evil.[1] Our feet can walk lightly—the burden of our sin has been lifted. We rejoice and thank God for all God has done, and fix our thoughts on what is true, honorable and right. Contentment can grow deep in our bones because our soul has been reconciled to God. Creation is being restored, and will ultimately be fully restored. Contentment, hope and peace flow from the comfort of knowing that God is the Victor, even as the earth groans for the coming restoration (Rom 8:19-22).

The Hebrews are told to be content with what they have. The author of the New Testament letter to them then writes:

"For God has said,

'I will never fail you.

I will never forsake you.'

That is why we can say with confidence,

'The Lord is my helper,

so I will not be afraid.

What can mere mortals do to me?'" (Heb 13:5-6).

Hebrews was written to the first-century church when persecution of Christian Jews threatened its very existence. We, like they, are encouraged to hold fast to faith while remembering the sufficiency of God's love to overcome evil in a violent world, to be an ever-present help, and to transform us into people who love and live rightly. Contentment is possible because of the work of Jesus Christ.

The Hebrews were to be content with what they had, even if that meant persecution and death. God desires the same for us, whatever good or ill may come. When we pursue contentment and savor life, we are saying that God is good, God is the Victor, and God will not leave us nor forsake us, even in the midst of chaos and trouble. We have nothing to fear. Our soul is safe. We can welcome a life tapestry woven with threads both painful and joyous, because we are loved and held by a personally present God.

Early on in life I decided I wanted to learn this art of savoring life. Mostly it was for practical reasons. Some old people had faces that wrinkled into smiles instead of frowns, and I wanted one of those when I grew old. I figured I needed to learn at a young age what it took to get one, so I started watching how people lived. People responded to everyday life differently, and I decided I'd rather be like Charlie (a friend of our family who had a face already destined to wrinkle into smiles in another twenty years) than like my third-grade teacher, Mr. Neal. Everyone loved Charlie, who generally loved life. His eyes looked like mischief waiting to happen. No one liked Mr. Neal, who didn't seem to like anyone or much of anything.

Then there was Uncle Jerry, who laughed a lot, embraced life and paid me quarters to tell my other uncles that he was my favorite. His face has learned to wrinkle into smiles. Some, like my piano teacher Mrs. Johnson, oozed gentleness. She looked right at me when we talked, and she listened with her whole body, engaging me and my lonely junior high life while we waited for my mother to pick me up after my lesson. I saw my father take delight in things like a horned toad sunning on a rock in Arizona, or shooting stars, or a cold glass of sun-brewed iced tea on a hot summer day. Gradually I learned that life hadn't been easy for those folks, but they had found ways to savor it just the same—not perfectly, and not always, but enough so that they had become contented souls that blessed those around them. They inspired me.

Sometime later I also learned that savoring life is bigger than me savoring *my* life. I belong to something much larger than myself. We all belong to God and each other, to those who came before us, and to those who will follow. We are part of the glorious creation made by the hands, voice and Spirit of God. To savor life, then, is to savor more than just my life. It is to savor and hold as dear this entire magnificent, wonderful miracle of God's creation.

For some the art of savoring life seems to come as naturally as breathing, but others of us have to learn it. I'm still learning to savor a world that's not the idyllic vision I once cherished. I think I am searching for Eden. I need reminding that contentment is rooted in the work of Christ and is to be experienced here and now in the small wonders, the miracles, evidence of redemption that is constantly unfolding around me.

Jesus showed God's love to us so completely and compellingly that we respond with gratitude. Jesus' life inspires, not simply by example but through a power to transform, enabling us to love God, others and creation as he did. Contentment flows from a life transformed and rightly lived. I value contentment, am called to be content and am finding joy in striving toward that obedience.

Learning any skill requires three things: gaining some relevant knowledge, learning the appropriate component skills and then practicing. In the following pages I explain how principles of contentment have been understood and practiced throughout history, explore how those principles can be applied to the particular challenges of our cultural context, and then encourage our taking up the practice of contentment—of savoring life.

But no matter how much we practice or how good we get at it, it's important to know up front that our soul will never be completely satisfied. We are eternal creatures made to experience something deeper and wider than our present earthly existence can satisfy. Full contentment will always elude us. So long as we live between Eden and heaven, we will yearn for something more.

Central to developing the art of savoring life is holding a hope that what our soul longs for will be satisfied someday. Hope helps us accept disappointment and even suffering, with the knowledge that God is present and will ultimately heal the wounds of a broken and distorted world, fulfilling the desires and longings of wounded and broken people. Meanwhile we relish the smell of autumn, an outdoor summer concert or a walk with a good friend. And hope strengthens its hold on our soul as we buy lunch for a homeless woman and work toward social change that will leave fewer children, women and men homeless. In so living we express a yearning for *shalom*—the peace experienced when the sun rises and sets on a world that is right and just. Contentment expresses hope in *shalom*. We listen to, mourn with and work to respond to cries for justice and redemption, while celebrating what is already beautiful and in the process of being restored.

I am a sociologist, one of those people who makes observations about how popular trends and sweeping social movements influence the way people come to think about themselves and then justify, organize and live out their lives. We look at personal choices people make in light of how a particular time and place in history has defined and shaped public issues and social troubles. Writing in the 1950s, sociologist C. W. Mills called this the "sociological imagination."[2] The permission to observe in this way—to observe and to connect the dots between personal experiences, social trends and public issues—drew me to sociology. I wanted to know how it happens that justice and *shalom* sometimes characterize a family, community, society or nation, though injustice and strife are generally so common. And how do beliefs affect behavior, so that some cultures came to place such a high value, for example, on technology and consuming?

Sociologists can be a cynical bunch—critiquing social structures, looking for hidden and not-so-hidden power struggles, exploring the interplay between the haves and the have-nots. Perhaps as an adult I needed to revive my childhood interest in happy souls because the discipline of sociology can incline me to despair. I need to be led back time and again to a transcendent hope that roots me in what is good and hopeful and beautiful about life. I want to be a contented soul that savors life in the midst of its ruin as well as its beauty.

Finding our way back requires realizing that we easily lose our way. We need to think carefully about where we want to be and determine whether we are on a road that will take us there. In *Mere Christianity*, C. S. Lewis summarizes the challenge before us:

We all want progress. But progress means getting nearer to the place where you want to be. And if you have taken a wrong turning, then to go forward does not get you any nearer. If you are on the wrong road, progress means doing an about-turn and walking back to the right road; and in that case the man who turns back soonest is the most progressive man. . . . And I think if you look at the present state of the world, it is pretty plain that humanity has been making some big mistake. We are on the wrong road. And if that is so, we must go back. Going back is the quickest way on.[3]

Wanting to learn the art of savoring life, I started hunting down contented souls. Some are alive and well and told me their own stories. I learned some by reading biographies or reading their own thoughts written down long ago. None of them are perfect people—they all have weaknesses, foibles and sins—and this gives me hope. The glory of God has shone through their human frailty as they learned to walk with contentment.

As I watched, read and listened to the stories of contented souls, theories of atonement kept emerging as points of connection. Many of them are trying to live the Good Life, a moral life, a life exemplified by love. They tend to live with hope, believing God is already the Victor and miracles happen. And finally, they live with peace—souls reconciled to and loved by God, who promises never to leave or forsake us. An ability to accept suffering, a consistent movement toward authentic connection with others, and holding to the hope for *shalom* characterize many whose contentment has seeped deep into their bones.

This book, then, is the culmination of my observations and reflections on the art of savoring life, clustered into eight characteristics of contented souls. Contentment that goes deep into our bones comes from placing our final hope in something yet to come, refusing to believe that all we'll get is whatever we can squeeze out of our seventy years or so on earth. So finding contentment starts with recognizing that we are souls that belong, rather than "consumers" (chapter two). Maintaining a posture of contentment takes fortitude, a willingness to sometimes embrace or sit with struggle rather than to be in a frenzy to escape it (chapter three). Contented souls exhibit a life-giving mellowness of heart (chapter four) that invites and welcomes rather than asserts or demands. Stretching toward contentment sometimes involves recognizing that we have lost our way and that finding it again takes a turning of sorts—accepting some limits on what has become a limitless life (chapter five). Those with contented souls are nourished by their ability to live intentionally—to look for small wonders, inhaling and absorbing the rich fullness that breathes around us, that is part of our very existence (chapter six), and they see through the superficialities of our consumer-driven life and desire to walk gently, to live as Jesus would live, mindful of all life, aware of our life-sustaining connection to the earth on which we live (chapter seven). The contented souls I have observed recognize the blessing that comes from belonging to others, from welcoming obligations and nurturing relationships despite living in a climate that encourages us to focus instead primarily on careers, acquisitions or achievements (chapter eight). And finally, contented souls remember. They are mindful of the past, of God's ongoing sustenance and plan for redemption, and their place in the long stream of humanity from which their life came (chapter nine).

Quakers have a tradition of using queries to prompt us toward deeper reflection about our lives. Following that tradition, I offer "queries for further reflection" at the end of each chapter for those who want to move beyond reading to journal, discuss or practice a life more characterized by contentment. You may want to journal responses to any question or questions that resonate with you, or use the questions in small group discussions with others reading alongside you.

May these pages call us to a contentment rooted in a God who loves us and calls us to be present to our earthy, physical existence as we journey toward *shalom*. Come walk with me. Let's kick up some leaves and later sip coffee—or tea or hot cocoa—while we savor the remains of the day and contemplate the presence of God in the quiet of our candlelit room.

QUERIES FOR FURTHER REFLECTION

- What drew you to this book? What do you hope to get out of it?
- Do you have particular expectations for what this book *should* say about contentment? Are you willing to be challenged in how you think about contentment, and how you live—to even, perhaps, be made uncomfortable?

SEEING THE SELF
AS SOUL

And the LORD God formed man of the dust of the ground, and breathed

into his nostrils the breath of life; and man became a living soul.

Pamela gathers people into her life—strangers, neighbors and kin. She seeks out, invites, welcomes and loves. We who know her have benefited from her choice to see the best in us, minimizing our faults and focusing on our strengths. To her we are not mere people but living souls.

A number of years ago, during a season that was stormy for both of us, Pamela told me she was realizing that joy is found most assuredly in the arms of God. She had spent too much time in previous years looking for it in people and relationships, and holding such high expectations that disappointment was inevitable. I resonated with her words and decided to spend a year meditating on that phrase. I started by making a pillow on which I stenciled, "Contentment is found in the arms of God." Authentic connections and contentment, I began learning that year, come from seeing ourselves as a soul that belongs not to our own self but to God, who made us and who loves us.

To see ourselves as a soul that *belongs* is to accept an invitation to hold life, relationships and possessions loosely, hands open, recognizing that nothing is really ours but that we belong to God and to all that is around us—our family, neighborhood, communities of work and worship, our country, our neighbors in the world, and the earth that sustains us all. A soul that belongs is a contented soul living in a place of quiet joy, and it invites, welcomes and calms those who draw near.

However attractive the image of a contented soul is to us, trying to escape the thorns and thistles of our existence is a natural response for human souls living in a physical world. As we grew increasingly able to manipulate our physical environment, we replaced the long-held belief that contentment comes from inside our soul with the idea that it comes from controlling our circumstances. Pursuing comfort and pleasure has become increasingly attractive since happiness was defined as personal ease and well-being—accessible through inventions, therapies, experiences and entertainment.

We forget that God is the source of our life, freedom and contentment. Hoping to escape hardship, we lean toward faith in a progress that is to bring greater comfort, health and productivity. But in the shadows of progress is a consumer-driven market eager to shape our desires and replace contentment with an insatiable hunger. Instead of living souls, we have become avid consumers.

THE UNMAKING OF THE SOUL

It has become popular of late to talk about the soul. But we do so casually, in a chicken-soup-for-the-soul kind of way. The soul is perceived as the touchy-feely part of our humanness, not to be taken too seriously but to be pampered from time to time, perhaps with chocolate, or a shopping spree, or a day of golf.

Throughout medieval times people were referred to as "souls," implying that we are eternal beings accountable to and belonging to God. Dallas Willard defines the soul as that dimension of a person that interrelates all other dimensions so that they form one life. The soul organizes our whole person: our mind and will, thoughts and feelings, body and social context, and through these "reaches ever deeper into the person's vast environment of God and his creation."[1]

I appreciate how the King James Version reminds us of our soulness: "And the LORD God formed man of the dust of the ground, and breathed into his nostrils the breath of life; and man became a living soul" (Gen 2:7 KJV). Newer translations replaced the word *soul* with "person," "being" or "creature." Episcopalian minister and psychiatrist Jeffrey Boyd says biblical theologians and philosophers of the twentieth century were concerned that use of the word *soul* had encouraged a body-soul dualism that focused overly much on the immortality of the soul. To correct what they thought was a denial of the body, they worked to remove the term *soul* both from Scripture translations and from common language used to describe personhood.[2] But in the process we may have lost an understanding of what it means to be living souls grounded in a physical world held together by a spiritual one. True freedom, according to Augustine, is the ability to choose to do what is right because body, mind and soul are fully aligned in a way that honors God, bringing us joy and contentment. The body and soul are not in competition but together move us ever deeper into the "vast environment" of God and creation.

The process of unmaking the soul didn't start in the twentieth century. Since the Fall we have been prone to separate the body and soul, usually attending more to the care and pleasure of our body. I admit, I'd rather sleep than keep a prayer vigil, and I'd rather eat than fast. And I'm not alone in this: the weight of history is on my side. We have generally welcomed worldviews and inventions that freed us from what we believed were rigid and superstitious rituals that put the body under submission to the soul as dictated to us by religious authority.

FROM SOUL TO SELF

The Enlightenment was one worldview that radically changed our sense of self. During the Enlightenment, freedom came to be understood as self-determination. The goal of life in Western societies shifted from serving God because God is the source of freedom and joy to serving the self because we are responsible to create our own pleasure and fulfillment. We stopped trusting that God has our joy in mind and entertained the possibility that God is in fact an authoritarian enemy of our joy. Gradually we just stopped believing that God has much to do with us at all. The upshot was that an individual's ability to apply reason to decisions about how to live and what is true came to be preferred over deferring to any claim of authority and revelation.[3]

This shift made sense in a fallen world, an effort to correct gross inequalities and injustices that decided people's fate solely by the accident of their birth. Throughout history the masses often lived with little freedom, autonomy or personal worth. Scripture, history and current world events are full of examples of how those with power have abused and exploited the masses who lack it. Kings, landowners, dictators, conquerors, world powers and multinational corporations easily took (and take) advantage of powerless people. Men, women and children were and are sold into slavery, forced into military service, treated as expendable biological units, trafficked in the sex trade and killed because they come from the wrong ethnic group or religion. Traditional authority, especially when infused with religious authority, has sometimes abused and oppressed those without power. So dictatorships and monarchies were struck down and replaced with democracies intending to give equality and voice to all. Theoretically every person was created equal, everyone mattered, and all would be represented in government and given political freedom to determine their own destiny, to make life better for themselves and their children.

My mother's parents were poor German immigrants who farmed

mostly sugar beets in Colorado. Grandma finished school through grade four, and Grandpa through grade eight. My aunts and uncles, born between 1912 and 1930, all graduated from high school. Two graduated from college, and two more attended for a couple of years before World War II took them off to war. They, and now my cousins' generation, climbed out of the lower rungs of typical immigrant poverty. Their experience exemplifies how meritocracy, a system intended to reward and encourage individual effort, has accompanied democracy in many parts of Western Europe and North America. Tragically, not all people in the United States gained equality and voice, particularly African Americans, Mexicans and Native Americans, who were conquered or exploited through colonization, but equality and self-determination were the stated values on which democracies and capitalism laid their foundation. People were expected to make life better for themselves and their children, however they defined "better," and the dominant majority was given adequate reason to believe it could be done.

Beginning in the late nineteenth century, social scientists like American sociologist Charles Cooley sought to understand and explain how a "self" develops. Cooley saw the self as constantly being shaped through interaction. For better or worse, we become selves in the context of our relationships with parents, friends, lovers, children and those in authority over us or under us. The Austrian founder of psychology, Sigmund Freud, also studied and therapeutically treated the self. Freud's theories were well accepted in a culture that wanted to believe in the "self-made man." Like Cooley, Freud saw the self as fated to be determined by its connections to others, but the therapeutic goal was to break the power of early dysfunctional attachments. According to Freud, people have the capacity to be self-determining, remaking themselves into whatever they choose. The pursuit of self-actualization and self-fulfillment replaced sacrifice and self-denial, now believed to come from unhealthy desires to please others. For most social scientists of the twentieth century, any belief in an eternal soul that belongs to God and is obligated to others should be kept within the private, preference-based realm of religion and out of the public domain. The autonomous self was born.

The fight to uphold the dignity and individual worth of every human is important, and numerous wars against nations and battles against multinational corporations have been fought in the name of freedom. All souls belong to a common humanity. We sin against humanity if in idolizing the autonomous self we disregard other souls. Fighting for justice, freedom and the individual worth of everyone requires remembering that we are all creatures belonging to God, accountable to others and most content when we live rightly—in ways that honor God and others.

FROM SELF TO CONSUMER

We struggle with balance. Our economic system doesn't help us here, because it makes contentment largely unobtainable. As self-determining people, we have become the center of our personal universe, and contentment depends on our ability to manage our identity, circumstances and life successfully. Companies provide us with new and improved products intended to help us be self-determining—and to make and remake our identity. We have become consumers and establish our status and identity by what we wear, use, drive and live in.

I started graduate school the year my youngest daughter started first grade. The prior decade I had been in maternity clothes or the casual clothes of a mother orchestrating the lives of three young children. Now I did what all self-respecting slightly older students returning to school did in the early 1990s—I bought myself a pair of Birkenstocks. Birkenstock wearers ate granola, grew vegetables, voted liberal, and liked trees and folk music. That fit me well enough—and so I established and showcased my identity with the shoes I purchased and wore.

I didn't need the Birkenstocks; I bought them to help shape my identity. And I am not alone. While economist Thorstein Veblen introduced the term "conspicuous consumption" to describe how the affluent used money at the turn of the twentieth century, it now also describes buying patterns of the middle classes.[4] Conspicuous consumption is pathological purchasing—a cycle of buying more than we need, then using, discarding and buying anew, not because we need it to live well but because it is the expected way to live. All who can afford to do so establish their identity by the clothes, cars, entertainment choices, electronic toys and vacations they purchase and consume. Consumption has become a way to define a soul now bereft of an identity outside itself, lost in the transition to autonomous self.

The transition from "soul" to "self" changed contentment from an internal state dependent on one's connection to God into an external state pursued through self-determining choices aimed at satisfying one's desires and dreams. The market plays with our desires. We become convinced that our fantasies and dreams could be satisfied with the products it offers. Transitioning from "self" to "consumer" is a natural next step, since it suggests that contentment is achieved primarily through experiences and products that can be purchased and consumed. A capitalist economy *depends* on keeping people discontented, so that they will keep buying the new and improved products that drive a burgeoning economy.

I have a wristwatch that belonged to my father's mother. The watch is an intricate work of art, inlaid with stones and designed to last a lifetime. My grandmother owned two or perhaps three watches over the course of seventy years. I can't count how many I have owned. Even a timepiece, once given as a significant gift worthy of being passed down to other generations, has become just one more exchangeable accessory we add to countless others in our wardrobe. Computers, cell phones and PDAs grow old the day we purchase them. (I had to look up PDA, which, in case you don't know, stands for "personal digital assistant." There is

something decidedly wrongheaded about calling an electronic gadget a
personal assistant—regardless of how *digital* it is!) We replace old but
functional appliances with more energy-efficient ones that offer more
programmable options and a fresh style. We (and I have been guilty
here) replace our adequate homes with bigger or better ones for sale in
other neighborhoods.

If we became content, we would stop purchasing, and our economy
would stop booming. Contentment may be good for the soul, but it is
bad for the economy. So styles change—not because we need to retire
the sleek look, the boxy look or the color avocado green, but because a
market economy feeds off people's purchasing power in a never-ending
search for contentment.

We have, by divine intention, an insatiable longing to belong, to have
an identity in something bigger than ourselves. In the absence of a strong
message that our identity and contentment come from being souls that
belong to God, we are easily persuaded that we can find some measure
of identity and belonging by what we consume. Marketers are depend-
ing on it. Books like *Emotional Branding: The New Paradigm for Connecting
Brands to People*[5] and *Designing Brand Identity: A Complete Guide to Creating, Building, and Maintaining Strong Brands*[6] instruct marketers of any
product or service how to get brand loyalty from customers. They have
been so effective that we pay for the privilege of being walking advertising agents. We are convinced that driving a particular brand of car
(maybe a Ford Explorer or Bronco with the "Eddie Bauer Edition" em-
blem glued to the side) or wearing shirts with "GAP" or "Abercrombie"
in big letters across the chest or down the sleeve is cool—that it gives us
an identity, a place to belong. Our conspicuous consumption says something about the kind of person we want to be as we announce that we
are a Gap or A&F or Eddie Bauer sort of soul.

People are often referred to as consumers, buyers, users or owners,
and we are not particularly struck by the oddity of it. "Increasingly own-

ers are preferring cats to dogs," or "Fifty percent of all buyers prefer decaf," or "Fifteen percent of consumers say they prefer talking on a cell phone." No longer are we autonomous selves; now we are consumers that can be manipulated by various market forces intent on convincing us that their products will give us the contentment for which we search.

And we are easily convinced. Since we already think of ourselves as autonomous selves who are supposed to craft our own happy life, it is easy to come to believe that contentment depends on our ability to choose and consume the right goods and services. Advertising provides a built-in mechanism to produce dissatisfaction. Campaigns emerge to convince consumers that life will be better today if they purchase products that didn't exist yesterday.

In the twenty-first century we are increasingly bombarded with advertisements from all directions—on buses, billboards, newsprint, television, radio, in shopping malls, arriving unbidden in our e-mail folders and popping onto our computer screens. In 1960, nine-and-a-half minutes per hour of prime-time television were devoted to commercials. By 2002, it had increased to fifteen minutes per hour.[7] Every time we pass someone on the sidewalk drinking from a Starbucks cup or carrying a bag from Target, Victoria's Secret or Nike, we are the recipient of subtle advertising encouraging us to identify ourselves with certain companies and then to buy, spend, consume.

Fifteen years after staking my identity in Birkenstocks, I chose to identify with gas-conscious motorists. I purchased a Honda Metropolitan, and as many days during the year as the weather permits I ride my scooter to work and around town. It's cute, orange and white, and it gets one hundred miles to the gallon. I think I'm announcing that I care about the environment, but I fear I may just be offering free advertising for Honda, declaring that scooters are cool toys even for middle-aged women wealthy enough to afford them. In our economically driven society, we can hardly avoid being conspicuous consumers.

A particular challenge to marketers was how to get money, and subsequent product loyalty, from one of the largest and most receptive consumer groups—children, who actually watch television commercials and are easy to manipulate. Initiative Media, the world's largest communications management company, developed a system aimed at getting children to nag their parents to buy them products.[8] With the help of child psychologists, they studied types of nagging and their effectiveness and then developed commercials aimed to induce the type of nagging most likely to influence the kind of parent being targeted for a particular product. Lucy Hughes, director of strategy and insight for Initiative Media, said,

> We found, for example, a quarter of all visits to theme parks wouldn't have occurred unless a child nagged their parents. Four out of ten visits to places like Chuck E. Cheese's would not have occurred. . . . We saw the same thing with movies, with home video, with fast food. Children's influence on what products the parents are buying is huge.[9]

When asked if her company's tactics to manipulate children are ethical, Hughes said: "I don't know . . . [but the company's goal is] to move products, and if we . . . move products . . . then we've done our job."[10] In general a corporation's goal is to make money. They are crafting future consumers, not souls.

An unintended byproduct of our self-determining, productive, economically vibrant and enriched lives is that we forget who we are. We forget that we are souls. As souls we are created to enjoy that which is free and simple—being cooled by a summer breeze, the music of a brook, the fragrance of lilacs, the strength of our body's bending into some physical labor, friendship, grace. Free pleasures and good gifts are forgotten in the overmarketing of pleasure for purchase. Self as soul is lost in our emphasis of self-determination and consumption.

The autonomous individual with worth and dignity, who rightly belongs to itself, is a necessary corrective to worldviews that justify a few holding power and control over the rest. But by the twenty-first century we have overcorrected to the point of losing a language for the soul-that-belongs. We are disconnected people primarily obligated to our self alone.

Our challenge is to live with this paradox: we are self-determining, unique image-bearers of God who yet belong to and are being transformed by God. We have obligations to meet, and while it seems paradoxical, in meeting them we find contentment. We can reclaim our soulishness and refuse to let our body and desires become conduits for consumption. We can exchange an identity bound up in products for one that rests in the comfort of belonging to God, to others and to the earth from which we come.

REMAKING THE SOUL BY REMEMBERING GOD

We could not remember God if God were not already remembering us. In remembering to whom we belong, and the claim that belonging makes on us, we renew our sense of self as soul. Thomas Merton says the "remembering of God" that David refers to in the Psalms is the rediscovery, the surprise, as we recognize again that God remembers us. God is always present with us, and when we release ourselves to the God who knows us, our soul is capable of remembering God.[11]

God is not the enemy of our joy but created us for joy, to experience happiness, to be profoundly moved by creation, in our relationships and in our longing for a consummate union with God in eternity. That joyful response glorifies God. When we look to things and accomplishments as our sources for happiness, we undermine a longstanding Christian understanding that happiness is linked to and emerges from knowing and loving God, which takes place in our soul. From that place of contented rest we can engage, love and serve others.

At some point along the way I noticed how serving or celebrating within a community of others could move me beyond any disappointment or sorrow that had derailed me and could draw me into greater contentment. Not only is caring for others good for others, it does our own soul good. Entering a community gives me perspective. It reminds me that I am part of something much bigger than just me.

Marcy and I touched on this during one of our coffee conversations. She is a student struggling through the pain of creating a necessary distance in a relationship that had become unhealthy. Both people knew they needed distance, and it brought both of them pain to do what they believed was best for them and for others who loved them. When Marcy asked what she could do with the pain, I encouraged her to sit with it for a while, to let it be okay to be sad and to hurt, resisting the temptation to escape or fix the situation. She found some consolation in that thought. Still, later she returned to it and asked, "So is there anything I can *do,* or do I just need to let it be okay to hurt?"

I looked at her thoughtfully and then said, "Mostly, you just need to let it be okay to hurt." After pausing I added, "But here's an experiment you might want to try. Each day make a point of looking for blessing and to stretch outside your sadness by seeking to bless someone."

I used to try to ease my lonely soul by pampering it. I'd take a walk, soak in my tub, treat myself to an extra mocha. Marcy and I talked about how it is to live in a time where we are told to focus on taking care of ourselves when we are hurting—often by consuming or buying something, activities that may bring some measure of comfort but mostly only hide our sadness for a while. Taking care of ourselves is good, but by itself it does not ease the loneliness that seeps into our soul when we are discouraged. Eventually I learned that what eases my lonely soul more than pampering it is blessing someone else. So after taking my walk or soaking in my tub, I will bake zucchini bread and give it away, using the fall's harvest kept grated in my freezer. Or leave a thank-you note with some cookies for the Ukrainian woman who cleans my office at night, or stop and talk to the folks painting the hallway, empathizing with the challenge of painting amidst the constant traffic of students and faculty.

We are created to derive pleasure and contentment from seeing the world as God sees it, to love it as God loves it, and to care for and enjoy others, God's creation and ourselves. As our soul enjoys God, we will enjoy life. Because the world is broken, we will not experience the full joy we were created for, but because our contentment comes from an awareness of a personal, ever-present God, we can rest in contentment even when our circumstances include suffering and loss.

Maya Angelou tells a story of her grandmother, a store- and property-owning black woman in Stamps, Arkansas, who offered grace in return for disrespect from children of poor white folks living on her property. Angelou's grandmother would stand on the porch softly humming hymns while the children mocked her in her front yard. She answered their questions respectfully and wished them well as they left. Describing the aftermath of one such encounter, Angelou wrote:

> She stood another whole song through and then opened the screen door to look down on me crying in rage. She looked until I looked up. Her face was a brown moon that shone on me. She was beautiful. Something had happened out there, which I couldn't completely understand, but I could see that she was happy. Then she bent down and touched me as mothers of the church "lay hands on the sick and afflicted" and I quieted.[12]

Angelou's grandmother was a contented soul. She lived graciously, knowing to whom she belonged and from where her value came. She could continue to stand on the porch humming because her pleasure and contentment were not wrapped up in trying to control her circumstances but in knowing to whom she belonged. So she returned a curse with blessing. Perhaps she saw herself as a soul who loved the broken world as God loves it and chose to define freedom as following the heart of God. Understanding that her capacity to arrange for happy circumstances was limited, she found a better way to live.

Contented souls recognize that they belong, and in that realization, they are free from the expectation that they craft their own perfect world. Seeing ourselves as a soul does not mean we become the doormat for a world ready to take advantage of us. Souls must take care of themselves so that they can do the work of taking care of others and of the world entrusted to us. Souls do not look out for themselves as an end in itself (as much as I may want to believe it, I am not, after all, number one), but so they can fulfill the claims made on them by God, the community and the world to which they belong. In meeting those claims, in doing what we were created to do, the soul learns fortitude, becomes mellow-hearted and open to limits, and begins to find contentment and satisfaction.

QUERIES FOR FURTHER REFLECTION

- The phrase *Cogito ergo sum,* "I think, therefore I am," given to us by seventeenth-century French philosopher René Descartes, had a profound influence on Western thought. However, it doesn't fit how the Bantu of South Africa understand personhood. Transposed into Bantu, the statement is "I am related, therefore I am." What does the Bantu statement add to an understanding of your sense of self and belonging?

- How has product branding affected your sense of identity and belonging? What clothes brands, restaurants, cars and companies do you most identify with, given your purchasing choices, and what do these brands represent for you? What would it look like for you to disengage from brand loyalty? What benefit would it bring your soul?

- For parents: How much are your children exposed to marketing? To what kinds of nagging are you most vulnerable? For example, "Everyone else has one; I need it to fit in," or "Mandy's/Matt's parents bought her/him one" (implying that if you love your child, you will buy this for him/her). How might you lessen their exposure to marketing and your susceptibility to their pleas?

- What is comforting about thinking you are a soul that belongs? What is comforting about thinking you are an autonomous self? What is *uncomfortable* about each of these? How is your self-perception shaped by an economic system that primarily sees you as a consumer?

THE PRACTICE
OF FORTITUDE

Come then . . . let us be resigned to our frailty and dependence on God,
who would never reduce us to being unable to walk
on our own feet if he had not the mercy to carry us in his arms.

JEAN-PIERRE DE CAUSSADE

One by one our backpacks showed up on the airport baggage carousel. Five of us were going to be hiking a stretch in the White Mountains of New Hampshire.

Kate's arrived—a Very Heavy pack (I had warned her against this), with an extra stash of peanut-butter cups and Butterfinger bars to give her extra energy along the way. Rae's arrived too, with the Advil we hoped would carry her through a fever, swollen glands and a sore throat she'd been struggling with for a couple of days. Jana's came, and so did mine. But Megan's didn't show up. It contained our second tent, one-fifth of our food, our cooking skillet, some chocolate-chip cookies she had stayed up until after midnight making as a surprise for us, and all her personal gear.

We filed our missing baggage report and agreed on a place and time the next day for a courier to rendezvous with us at a trailhead, delivering the waylaid backpack. Being courageous, adventurous women (two seventeen-year-olds, a fourteen-year-old and two forty-year-olds), we resolved not to be discouraged.

Just as the last of the sunlight muted to gray, we left the car and started a steep ascent that stretched as far as we could see. Hiking in the dark was not in our original plan, but three hours of hiking by flashlight were required to reach our campsite. Once there, exhausted and a bit more discouraged than we wanted to admit, we put up our tent, packed three people inside our "three-person tent" (a description that was only technically correct) and tried to sleep. The two who had stayed outside squeezed in at four in the morning, driven by the cold. None of us slept well.

The next day we hiked four miles to Zealand Falls. Once there, the others napped or frolicked in the falls while Megan and I hiked the five-mile round-trip loop to meet the courier at the agreed-upon trailhead. Long after the window of time had elapsed for our rendezvous, there was no courier, thus no backpack, no tent, sleeping bag, clothes, gear or more food. But some gracious hikers finishing their trip asked for our story and in exchange gave us some leftover crackers, Nutri-Grain bars and trail mix. Their kindness gave us strength. We hiked back to join the others and then pushed on to finish what was for Megan and me a twelve-mile day.

And so a glorious endurance began. We shared our personal gear; Kate loaned Megan a second pair of socks, and she wore my long underwear as outerwear most of the week, using her pants (which she had ripped into shorts) for swimming and hiking on hot days. We had so much fun carving spoons from sticks that each of us later took home a memento of our ingenuity and sharing.

Another couple shared some food, and a ranger took pity on our plight and gave us directions to a secret pool, known as the "Ranger Swimming Hole" among the few rangers who knew of it. We had the pool all to ourselves. We swam, floated downstream with the current and napped on sun-kissed boulders.

Megan still got drenched in the rain, crossed streams in the only shoes she had, and went all week without brushing her teeth, changing her underwear or eating any of her specially mixed Gorp, known for its unusually high proportion of M&Ms. I'm thought of as a good trail cook, but the food we ate that week—the pancakes made in a borrowed skillet, our homemade dehydrated beef stew, carrot salad, and peanut-butter chocolate bars—tasted particularly superb because we were hungry and food was in short supply. The beauty of the sunsets, the night sky, and the mountain peaks and valleys were made more precious because of our various trials and shortages. We slept cold, went to bed hungry and enjoyed the week gloriously. We surrendered to circumstances we could not control and embraced the moments as they came.

When we embrace struggle, we dignify both our human strength and our frailty. We learn fortitude and what we are capable of enduring. And we open ourselves to receive blessings from others.

THE SECRET OF SURRENDER

The secret of surrender was spoken of in days before scientific progress gave us the illusion of control. The eighteenth-century writings of a little-known French Jesuit priest were compiled one hundred years later and published under the title *Self-Abandonment to Divine Providence*. The 1966 English translation is called *The Sacrament of the Present Moment*. Jean-Pierre de Caussade encourages Christians to recognize God in every moment—not to run from struggle but to surrender to it, trusting that God's will is found in our actions and our suffering. Caussade says:

> To discover God in the smallest and most ordinary things, as well

as in the greatest, is to possess a rare and sublime faith. To find contentment in the present moment is to relish and adore the divine will in the succession of all the things to be done and suffered which make up the duty to the present moment.[1]

Caussade's eighteenth-century world had not yet produced technologies capable of easing the hardships that characterized life for many. Our ability to alleviate pain and to eradicate many diseases and hunger for most members of our developed and wealthy countries influences our view of suffering. So I join a chorus of twenty-first-century Christians who want to soften Caussade's message—believing that God's will is less *that* we suffer, but knowing we will suffer, God promises to be present with us and give us strength to endure.

Walking with God in "the duty of the present moment" takes fortitude; the ability to stay in the moment, and to respond virtuously in it. To keep on keeping on. Rather than attempting to escape some unpleasant experience, I want to learn to rest in God, knowing that God desires my transformation, and would use this moment to help me see, understand and love more deeply. Instead of trying to fix all my discomforts, or escape boring, onerous or unpleasant tasks, I want to learn to respond virtuously in each moment, as is my obligation.

Throughout the early months of 2005, the world saw Pope John Paul II giving dignity to life with significant pain, responding virtuously and with fortitude as we watched him walk through his final days of suffering. When we treat each moment as sacred, we learn from one moment what will uphold some practice of virtue in the next. God uses every experience to shape, teach and prepare us. As followers of Christ, we are instructed to experience all of life deeply, holding on to the hope of God while being present to whatever *this* moment brings, because God is there. This is the secret of surrender.

We more easily sit with suffering, receptive to what God brings in difficult moments, if we trust that God is doing something transformative through the hardship. But it's hard to accept that human dignity might be tied to how we respond to our finiteness. Struggle teaches us resilience and hope. We would lose a fundamental strength of our humanity if we lost all need and ability to be resilient. In struggles we learn what we are capable of enduring, and in the process our humanity is dignified. Progress that eases struggle is good, yet the paradox is that struggle is also good, because it builds fortitude, the endurance that develops through hardship and difficulty. Struggle reminds us that we are not intended to live solitary lives but are necessarily embedded in community—we seek God in misery as well as joy and desire others in times of gladness and times of need.

STRUGGLE DIGNIFIES OUR HUMANITY

Christians believe human beings bear God's image, even when their bodies and lives are full of suffering. The summer before beginning his senior year at Wheaton North High School, Dave was diagnosed with a brain tumor. He and his family pursued medical treatments, but the diagnosis suggested that a miraculous healing would be required for Dave to graduate. Dave, a football player, continued to show up for Friday night games to cheer the team on from the sidelines. At first he walked with help; eventually he was rolled into place in his wheelchair. As long as he was able, he attended classes and kept up with his friendships.

He hadn't yet been baptized and wanted to participate in this sacrament to give witness to his life of faith. As he was losing the ability to speak clearly and recognized that he might not be able to speak the words on his heart at his baptism, he had his testimony videotaped a few weeks ahead of time. He spoke powerfully of his faith, his love of God, and his desire that his life and his death would bring God glory. Dave told his family that he was okay with dying, especially if through his death someone else might come to know Jesus.

He died a few weeks before graduation. During the graduation ceremony for the class of 2002, the principal called Dave's name when his turn would have come, and his parents went forward to receive his diploma. His fellow students and the parents of his classmates gave Dave a standing ovation—a testimony to a boy who had lived well and struggled faithfully to the end.

Believing human life was sacred, Dave, a seventeen-year-old boy, died with dignity and integrity. It took courage and fortitude. God calls us to surrender to these most difficult moments, and in the surrender to find contentment.

The problem of suffering has always challenged Christians struggling to understand how an all-loving and all-powerful God allows pain and evil. We have suffering that comes from natural causes and disasters and suffering that comes from people's choices. God created us with human agency—the capacity to choose to do good or evil—despite knowing such a world would include significant suffering. Theologian Daniel Migliore says that out of love for the world God entered it and walked among us, to experience our suffering, to embrace it in death, and to demonstrate God's victory over death and evil in the transforming power of the resurrection. Migliore summarizes the nature of God's power by saying it is

> the self-giving love of the creator, redeemer, and consummator of the world. The power of the triune God is not raw omnipotence but the power of suffering, liberating, reconciling love. . . . The God who creates and preserves the world is not a despotic ruler but "our Father in heaven"; not a distant God but a God who becomes one of us and accompanies us as the incarnate, crucified, risen Lord; not an ineffective God but one who rules all things by Word and Spirit rather than by the power of coercion.[2]

God's faithful love began with creation and continues through to a world that will ultimately be transformed and restored. We are called to partner with God to redeem what is broken in the world, in our own lives and in the lives of others. Dying is perhaps the ultimate struggle, but in living long and aging we inevitably experience significant suffering.

Lyle, a rather ordinary man living in a small town in Oregon, is responding to God's call to surrender his life as a witness to human dignity in the midst of human frailty. Lyle was a faithful Christian, active in our church, a good citizen, and a generous and kind man. All of us in the youth group liked and respected him. In the years since we graduated from high school and moved into adult life, Lyle began to face enormous professional, personal and physical pain that is now culminating in symptoms that reflect Parkinson's and Alzheimer's.

In his troubles, Lyle found and clung to a spirit of hope, striving toward joy and contentment in spite of his circumstances. In the early years his troubles regularly kept him awake for two or three hours in the middle of the night, his mind churning, frustrated, mad and upset because God was allowing unjust things to happen. Eventually he went to a good friend, who encouraged him to search the Scripture for teachings on suffering. One passage that became particularly significant to him was Philippians 4:4-9. Lyle says:

> Paul tells us to practice certain things if we want to have the peace of God. We are to rejoice in the Lord always even if life is tough and I might be in jail unjustly. We are told to let our forbearing spirit be known to all, and not to be anxious about anything, because a just God is near and watching. We are instructed to be thankful while lifting our prayers to God, and to replace wrong thinking and erroneous blame with meditation about things that are true, honorable, right, pure, lovely, of good repute, and worthy of praise. God says if I practice these things both the "God of peace" and the "peace of God" will be with me. And as I began

practicing God brought ever-increasing contentment in the midst of my circumstances. I am learning to "count it all joy when I encounter various trials knowing that the testing of my faith produces endurance and maturity" (Jas 1). I choose to see value in suffering because I know that my "suffering produces perseverance; perseverance, character; and character, hope. And hope does not disappoint" (Rom 5:3-5). These are not just verses from a book; they are promises being proved true as I exercise them. So I choose contentment. I choose to learn to reject anger, and accept the peace of God.

When I asked him about his Alzheimer's symptoms, he told me that his mind "disconnects" at times. The first was when he couldn't remember his wife's name in a social setting. Another time in a meeting he experienced his mind "as if in a big dark room with no possibility of connecting to anyone or anything." He described a day he became lost while driving down a highway that was as well known to him as the street in front of his home. To deal with the frustration and fear of these moments, Lyle trained himself to focus on a memorized verse and think about its implications. When he does this, he calms and is able to move away from negative and despairing thoughts toward positive ones. His lifelong commitment to practice at joy and contentment are serving him well during this current trial.

Everyday annoyances that we call "pain" give us opportunity to practice at joy and contentment that transcend our circumstances, to learn from the minor aches that can prepare us for greater suffering. When we let the pain of our body speak to us (back pain, migraine headaches, menstrual cramps), we are treating our humanity in all its frailty and beauty with dignity. Pain can give us an increased sensitivity to a world that seems both beautiful and askew. In pain we often desire quiet and want to be alone. When we pull away to remember, reflect, pay attention and allow ourselves to grieve a body that yearns for redemption, we give dignity to our soul—attending to the moment, embracing our humanity.

I take Advil when my joints ache; I'm not against taking medication. But could we be more mindful of our physical existence, not always rush to eradicate discomfort but embrace bodies that are responding to a broken world that cries out for redemption?

Depression is a sensitive example. Neuroscience has taught us that serotonin and norepinephrine play an important role in the brain and that low levels of them are associated with depression. Once we understood the brain chemistry of depression, the pharmaceutical industry developed various antidepressants that combated the problem. This was largely a social good. *For people with severe depression, these are life-sustaining medications.* That cannot be emphasized enough, especially in a Christian culture that is predisposed to consider depression a spiritual condition. For those living in darkness, who cannot escape suicidal thoughts and despair, antidepressants can free them to function as healthy human beings whose brain chemistry is in balance.

However, Francis Fukuyama challenges the culture and pharmaceutical industry that encourage us to take antidepressants not because we are clinically depressed but because antidepressants can make us feel "better than good."[3] A state of normalcy gets defined by a medication that can make everyone feel "happier"; but some amount of sadness might be more appropriate, even more desirable, for the sake of our soul.

Numerous other examples can be cited. Harvard neurologist Thomas Scammel refuses to prescribe Modafinil, a drug that allows people to function without sleep, to those wanting to get more done by sleeping less.[4] The drug Viagra is coming to define "normal sexual desire" for men. While Viagra has its useful purposes for men suffering from significant dysfunction, it is being marketed as an enhancer of normal functioning, so that "normal" comes to be defined in very narrow terms. Seasonale, a drug that makes it possible for women to put their menstrual cycle on hold for three months at a time, reinforces the belief that the female body as it naturally functions is a nuisance and a burden and should be improved upon and enhanced.[5]

Fukuyama reminds readers of Aldous Huxley's 1932 science-fiction novel *Brave New World,* in which people resolve all physical or mental discomfort by taking one pill or another. Huxley's new world is indeed creepy: the mess and trouble of childbearing has been replaced by a technologically engineered form of "hatching," and life is defined by ease, clean to the point of sterility and lived in a state of drug-induced euphoria. In the early twenty-first century we mimic this fictional world far more than we would have dared to expect. We can put our faith in science and the development of stress-reducing technology, but in the process we may be altering something of what it has meant to be human throughout history.

What if God's image shines most brightly through our human nature in the midst of difficulties? If we were to eradicate all limits, pain and struggle, what hole would their absence leave in our human nature? Might we become incapable of bearing the weight of suffering or even disappointment? Psychologists and sociologists working with families have learned to encourage parents to resist the urge to pave too smooth a road for their children. Overindulged and overprotected children have a harder time coping with life's inevitable disappointments in adulthood. Might that also be true of us in adulthood if we seek to define "normal" as freedom from all hardship?

When we embrace the struggles of embodied souls making their way through life, we give dignity to a humanity crying out for redemption and receiving mercy. This is not glorifying pain, but it is acknowledging the frailty and limits of our humanity. In a willingness to embrace them, we can see what mercy and good may come through them.

So can we sit with some measure of sadness, some level of anxiety, some amount of sleeplessness, recognizing the world isn't the way it's supposed to be and our humanity feels it in its flesh and bones? There is a wise sadness that comes from recognizing how unlike paradise earth has become. We bring a kind of dignity to our embodied existence when we sit with our suffering, as Jesus did in the Garden of Gethsemane, and attempt to listen to the underlying woes, recognizing that no matter how much we attempt to assuage our discomfort, the contentment and fulfillment we long for will not be fully ours this side of eternity.

WE LEARN WHAT WE ARE CAPABLE OF ENDURING

On the White Mountains backpack trip, Rae learned that she was capable of strenuous hiking even with a sore throat, swollen glands and a slight fever. Mark was home worrying about her, fearing we might end up burying her alongside some mountain trail. It's a good thing he didn't know we were missing a fifth of our gear and food! But it felt like a once-in-a-lifetime trip; she wanted to go. She got better the third day and learned a lot about what she was capable of on that trip—and I learned it too. Even once she was healthy, I wasn't sure how she'd handle the hiking, as she hadn't done much of it before. But in the eight years since that trip, she has backpacked more than the rest of us combined. She, more than any of us, learned what her body could do, even under duress, and has taken good advantage of that knowledge.

In fact, a few years ago Rae was thinking about taking a six-week solo backpack trip. About that time the story of Aron Ralston, an experienced climber and outdoorsman on a nine-day solo trip, began circulating in the news. At the end of the trip he hiked five miles out of the Bluejohn Canyon with one arm less than he had when he started. Ralston had been pinned under an eight-hundred-pound boulder. After five days he figured he'd have to amputate his arm if he wanted to survive. He did, then rappeled down a sixty-foot cliff and hiked out of the canyon. I told Rae, "The moral of the story is, don't solo hike."

She said lightheartedly, "No, Mom, the *real* moral of the story is, humans have a great survival instinct and are incredibly innovative when they have to be."

Struggle helps us learn what we are capable of enduring. Ralston had solo hiked before and knew enough to carefully plan out every phase of his amputation before he began it. Undoubtedly struggle and hardship on earlier trips helped prepare him for this one.

We are strengthened through physical and emotional challenges. We become courageous, innovative and resourceful as we learn about the earth, our body and each other. It is tempting in this technologically advanced age to let others do all the innovating so that we can simply apply their knowledge of the earth and of human bodies to our various challenges. We don't have to reinvent the proverbial wheel. But a bit of courage and mastery foster contentment—the satisfaction of knowing how a thing works, how to repair it, what's edible in the wild, and what alternative one might have if, in a pinch (being pinned beneath an eight-hundred-pound boulder qualifies), one needs to be resourceful.

Where Did All the Cowboys Go?

By the turn of the twentieth century, some men were concerned that the kind of courage and resourcefulness used to settle the American West was dying out. The frontiers had been discovered, and the world had been largely civilized, colonized and industrialized. There wasn't much need for everyday folk to be courageous or resourceful anymore, and city life and sit-at-a-desk day jobs "feminized" or softened men, weakening the courage, skill and strength that had defined manhood. Out of his concern, in the late 1800s Daniel Carter Beard started the Society of the Sons of Daniel Boone, which became the Boy Scouts of America in 1910. Beard wrote books to encourage outdoor living and survival skills; in a 1914 Boy Scout document he wrote:

The Wilderness is gone, the Buckskin Man is gone, the painted Indian has hit the trail over the Great Divide, the hardships and privations of pioneer life which did so much to develop sterling manhood are now but a legend in history, and we must depend upon the Boy Scout Movement to produce the MEN of the future.[6]

Seventy-five years later, Robert Bly wrote *Iron John,*[7] the now-classic men's manifesto. Bly wrote in a post-Vietnam era to men disillusioned by the John Wayne stoicism and stiff upper lip they had tried to live by. Bly wanted men to feel a full range of emotions and to grieve lost connections with their fathers. He crafted a vision for manhood that borrowed from mythology, psychology, anthropology and sociology. Bly warned against the cage of duty and niceness and encouraged men to embrace their sexual hunger, wildness and natural strengths.

Bly attributed men's inability to embrace manhood to the Industrial Revolution. Men had left family-owned farms and businesses to work in factories or offices, leaving boys to be raised by mothers, no longer guaranteed side-by-side learning of diverse skills, strength and courage from their fathers. Bly mourned the loss of fathers who no longer taught their sons the skills and character qualities needed if they were to be courageous men. He propelled a men's movement forward with his mythopoetic writing and suggestions of rites and rituals to help men celebrate manhood.[8]

Ten years later, John Eldredge built on themes introduced by Bly and crafted the bestselling Christian book *Wild at Heart.*[9] Eldredge attributed the feminization of manhood to a church that encourages men to be nice, gentle husbands and fathers who stay home with their wife and children on weekends and vacation with the family at theme parks and resorts. In *Wild at Heart* he challenges men to find their manhood in God's image, to rediscover their dreams of being heroes, to become passionate and powerful adventure seekers.

In other contexts there is much I would challenge in the assumptions of both Bly and Eldredge. Here, suffice it to say that responses to their books, and the popularity of war movies and movies with heroes like *Braveheart*'s William Wallace and Maximus in *Gladiator*, indicate that people are drawn to stories of the courageous.

Most of us inhabiting the middle class live public lives of relative safety and ease.[10] Except for soldiers in times of war and some police officers and firefighters, few of us have jobs requiring us to bravely confront significant danger and death. Civilization, democracy and technological advances have all contributed to a life that requires little physical courage. Bly and Eldredge would have men create adventures to fill an unmet craving for something that requires courage.

I don't doubt that we need courage and that many of us would enjoy an adventure every now and then. But always, more than courage, humans have needed and still need fortitude.

Thomas Aquinas spoke of courage as having two aspects: an aggressive element and an enduring one. He saw the endurance element, which he called fortitude, as the higher virtue. Philosopher Albert Borgmann calls fortitude the mental and patient side of confronting danger and trouble, while courage is the physical and daring side.[11]

Fortitude is required of single mothers working minimum-wage jobs to support themselves and their children. And it takes fortitude to challenge a worldview that suggests a consumer-driven, individualistic, materialistic lifestyle defines the abundant life God intended us to enjoy. When we uphold virtue, stand against the status quo, and resist ease and ignorance by challenging widely held assumptions, we exercise fortitude. Completing any arduous task—getting oneself up and off to work, or taking care of children, or studying diligently, or "keeping on keeping on" when every day feels full of trouble—is an exercise in fortitude.

Frodo Baggins and Samwise Gamgee are the unlikely heroes of J. R. R. Tolkien's *Lord of the Rings* trilogy. Hobbits like to keep to themselves, let the world unfold around them and not get caught up in the affairs of human beings, elves, dwarfs and wizards. Yet Frodo and Sam are swept up in an adventure that requires them to leave their comfortable hobbit holes and lose the veil of ignorance that allowed them to enjoy a quiet pastoral life.

They are selected for their fortitude, not their courage. Part of what people love about the story is how these two hobbits persevere, despite their hobbit frailty, on a journey to Mount Doom to destroy a ring that would destroy the world. They do not give up, and that, most of all, is what is required of them. No one expects them to kill orcs, goblins or the powerful Nazgul, servants of the Dark Lord. They are required only to faithfully journey along a path that will include hardship, require perseverance and call forth all their physical, mental and emotional strength. So they continue to put one hairy foot in front of the other as they cross the desert of Mordor. Sam carries Frodo when he no longer has strength to walk. When Frodo grows weak or weary under the weight of his burden, Sam keeps him mindful of the importance of the task before them. They exude fortitude.

What Tolkien tapped in a story that has captured the imaginations of readers for fifty years was this: when struggle exposes our human frailty, the strength of character that emerges is worthy of praise. Many of us live in hobbitlike neighborhoods where we can keep to ourselves, letting the world unfold as it will, outside our borders. Yet we are inspired by stories of heroes—those who emerge from their comfortable realm to exercise courage and fortitude for the sake of others.

We have daily opportunities to practice and build fortitude. When we choose to love another over ourselves, we are showing a moral fortitude that stands against the taken-for-granted principle of "looking out for Number One." When we forgo buying something we want but do not need, when we walk or bike instead of driving, or when we drive a smaller car, we are standing against a principle of consumerism and choosing a moral fortitude that is kinder to the environment, or better for our body, or will benefit our relatives, our next-door neighbors or our neighbors half a world away. We can give our extra money away instead of spending it now or saving it for later. We can say no to activities that keep us occupied but do not develop our capacity to love others, express gratitude or be responsible. Some of us would benefit from getting rid of televisions, cell phones and perhaps even our laptop computer so that we could be more mindful of living fully in the present moment. Resisting becoming mesmerized by a Me-First, Supersize-Me, You-Deserve-the-Best, Buy-Now-Pay-Later, It's-All-About-Me culture is practicing fortitude.

One of the booths at a farmers' market I frequent throughout the summer and fall is run by a family that tills, plants and harvests a small eight-acre farm. Five years ago the father had a job in the city; he rarely saw his children and felt driven to spend his energy on tasks that had little congruency with his values. So he and his wife decided to leave corporate America and try farming. They homeschool their children and teach them how to be intentional caretakers in touch with the land that sustains them. They sell soaps they have made from goat's milk and wool they have spun from the sheep they raise. They bring organic vegetables, free-range eggs and an alternative way to live in the world.

Financially it's been a hard choice. But they are living in harmony with their values. When fathers and mothers say, "I want to be present to my children," and then make sacrificial choices to make that possible, they are exercising fortitude.

There is a satisfaction, a contentment, that comes from mastery, from learning how to work the soil to produce succulent tomatoes or fragrant flowers, or to spin wool or make soap. Few of us will switch our life midstream and exchange a desk job for raising sheep and making soap. But we can all welcome small challenges or large ones, those requiring mental rigor, creative innovation or physical strength. In all of them, we gain an appreciation for what we are capable of enduring, learning, mastering.

And when we exercise fortitude, surprisingly, we often find we have

stepped onto a path that can lead to greater contentment. We are reminded of our capacity to withstand hardship and to live with moral fortitude, and of our dignity as finite human beings created in the image of
God.

THE BLESSING OF COMMUNITY

Hollywood lifted another hero from classic literary pages (that is, if one
can call Marvel Comics literary—or classic) at the same time Tolkien's
first *Lord of the Rings* movie was released. *Spider-Man* features Peter
Parker, an ordinary boy who becomes an extraordinary hero.

A significant difference separates these stories. Peter Parker acts alone;
Frodo acts in the company of friends. Peter saves the world by himself—
he is so alone that no one knows his identity. He forfeits love (as do all
superheroes) to save the world, but a superhero he will be, must be.

Frodo begins his journey traveling with companions, and he ends it
with a companion who will not let him carry on alone. The arduous task
of saving the world requires a fellowship—*The Fellowship of the Ring*, the
first book in the trilogy, is about the nine companions who set out to
help Frodo accomplish his task. The skills, interests and wisdom of all
of them are required for the mission to succeed. By the end of the journey, the faithful Sam is the only one still able to accompany him. Frodo
can't do alone what he has to do to save the world.

Herein lies a very liberating truth: we are created to be far more like
Frodo Baggins than like Peter Parker. We are to accomplish what we accomplish with companions, in the context of some community. We are
not intended to act alone.

Stoic individuals are uncomfortable showing weakness, reflecting the
staunch independence that characterizes our culture, particularly
among men but increasingly among women as well. I seldom ask anyone
except Mark for help with a project. In fact I can't imagine asking a
neighbor for a cup of sugar; I just go to the store to get my own. Mark is

worse than I am. He doesn't even ask *me* for help. He'll lift things alone that would be better lifted by the two of us and work on extensive construction projects alone, hiring help (he's rarely asked a friend to volunteer a few hours) only when it's absolutely necessary. We've noticed that since we aren't in the habit of asking for assistance, others also only rarely ask us for help. Perhaps by not asking for help, we subtly communicate "Bother not, that ye may not be bothered," even though we would gladly help others. At any rate, we are both working on this shared fault, with mild success.

Scripture is full of reminders that we are not intended to manage the challenges of life on our own. New Testament writer Paul admonishes us to fulfill the law of Christ by bearing one another's burdens (Gal 6:1-2). King Solomon says in Ecclesiastes 4:9-12:

> Two people can accomplish more than twice as much as one; they get a better return for their labor. If one person falls, the other can reach out and help. But people who are alone when they fall are in real trouble. And on a cold night, two under the same blanket can gain warmth from each other. But how can one be warm alone? A person standing alone can be attacked and defeated, but two can stand back-to-back and conquer. Three are even better, for a triple-braided cord is not easily broken.

Because we can buy burden bearers in the form of guidance, comfort and encouragement from counselors, life coaches and psychologists, we often miss opportunities to be present to each other, either in emotional pain or in physical hardship. We want neither to burden another nor, if most of us are honest, be overly burdened by another.

Yet we fulfill the law of Christ when we bear each other's burdens. We love each other as Christ loved us, laying down his life for us. As we do so, our stories are woven into a living tapestry of human struggle and perseverance in the context of a community. We open ourselves to blessing in our extended family, faith community, neighborhood or work community when we humble ourselves to need others and be needed by others.

EMBRACING STRUGGLE AND MERCY

At some points, or at many, each of us will be immersed in an experience of pain. God knew that in our fallen state we would need struggle and pain to keep us moving toward each other and toward God. And God's grace and mercy is always at work, redeeming what is broken, making a way through, bringing dignity and opportunities to learn in this moment what we need to be virtuous in the next.

Throughout history the human story has been characterized by an amazing capacity for courage, perseverance and holding on to hope in the face of great trouble. God has always been present in times of struggle and suffering. With Christ, whose strength is sufficient, we can choose, indeed we are obligated to choose, to live virtuously in difficult moments.

God has extended mercy to us by giving human beings the ability to learn, over the centuries, how to eradicate some of our misery and trouble. But eradicating misery is not a guarantor of contentment; actually our expectation for a life of ease increases our discontent when our expectations are unmet. When we accept struggle as part of living in a broken world and carry on rather than giving up, we are exercising fortitude. Fortitude, in turn, helps us embrace the mercy and grace that emerge from hardship. When we recognize the good of those God-given mercies, contentment has a chance to settle deep into our bones.

QUERIES FOR FURTHER REFLECTION

- How can you practice being mindful of ordinary moments today—perhaps as you eat a meal, walk from your car to the building you work in, converse with a colleague or a child? What keeps you from finding God "in the smallest and most ordinary things"?

- Can you use traffic frustration to practice responding virtuously in every moment? Becoming mindful in moments of frustration, can you stop, calm yourself and look for God in the midst of it? Can you let physical discomfort such as migraines and emotional discomfort from stress at work or home be a practice ground for responding virtuously to harder things to come?

- In what ways do you run from suffering? What would it look like to sit with it instead, as Jesus did in Gethsemane?

- What struggle(s) in life has (have) forged resilience in you?

- Are you more inclined to be a Peter Parker hero or a Frodo Baggins hero? Do you have a company of friends you are willing to call on? Who are they?

- Exercise: Take an inventory of skills you have that bring you satisfaction—for example, playing an instrument, playing a sport, gardening, fitness, cooking or baking, art. Which have been neglected of late? Choose one to practice again or a new one to learn.

MELLOWNESS OF HEART

God, grant me the serenity to accept the things I cannot change,

courage to change the things I can, and the wisdom to know the difference.

Living one day at a time, enjoying one moment at a time,

accepting hardship as the pathway to peace;

taking, as He did, this sinful world as it is,

not as I would have it;

trusting that He will make all things right

if I surrender to His will;

that I may be reasonably happy in this life,

and supremely happy with Him forever in the next.

REINHOLD NIEBUHR[1]

One semester in a Sociology of Family course I taught at Wheaton College, our discussion turned toward matters of misery and loss, though we fell upon the topic rather accidentally. We were talking about perceptions regarding family obligations and individual rights. I quoted the author of our text: "Can a person in a miserable marriage ever be a complete and effective parent to his or her children?"[2] We decided the question was somewhat wrongheaded but was understandable in a culture that puts a high premium on individual happiness. Barring situations such as abuse, can a married person accept less than desirable circumstances (a.k.a. "misery") and still be an effective parent? Is personal happiness the ultimate pursuit and end product against which all other successes or failures are to be measured?

We were trying to distinguish between trouble we accept and trouble we reject.[3] We wanted to explore the balance between accepting and "dealing with" hard circumstances on the one hand and rejecting them and fighting for change on the other. We decided our inclination as Westerners is not to accept much of any trouble—and to respond to all misery with some mix of anger or woundedness.

The class decided that the current trend was to live in a state of mild to moderate disgruntlement while constantly pursuing "happiness," defined as enjoying our circumstances. Though we press for happiness, often we are inclined to gain sympathy and permission to indulge ourselves by telling people we are miserable, busy, tired or stressed, proving that we have a high angst quotient. We tend to consider people with a low angst quotient to be shallow, not in touch with the deep pains of life and the looming questions that plague angst-ridden folks. When the optimists argue for focusing on the fullness of the proverbial cup rather than its emptiness, they are dismissed as naive, insensitive types likely to break out in Bobby McFerrin's song "Don't Worry, Be Happy" at the first signs of distress. McFerrin's angst quotient is clearly too low.

One student said, "Our culture glorifies victimization. It's expected that people are discouraged or hurt or offended about something, and it's expected to consume them. Sometimes people just need to get on with life." He gained some credibility from those who knew that his father had recently died and that, as an only child, he had been spending a fair amount of time traveling back and forth to Hong Kong to help his mother take care of things. He didn't mean to say one shouldn't grieve but that people should not stay stuck in a state of paralysis brought on by a culture overly focused on losses, pain and disappointments.

A student whose biological father had abandoned the family when he was a toddler, and whose stepfather had died four years back, said the whole conversation about allowing self-pity seemed irrelevant to him. He grew up in a family that always had to "just get on with life," whether it was rebounding from an abusive father who eventually deserted them or the death of a stepfather with whom he had never connected. Self-pity is a leisure only afforded the middle and upper classes, he said. The rest of the world just does what needs doing to keep life going.

After tiptoeing in and out of the subject for a while, I suggested we step back and look at the assumptions that shape our views. Namely, we are a culture focused on individual experience and our own pain, so that we feel betrayed if our friends suggest it is time to stop licking our wounds, get ourselves up and perhaps do someone else a bit of good. In fact, our Christian theology and the wisdom of the ancients suggest that attending to others may be our salvation out of our own misery. Enjoyment or happiness was never intended to be separated from living the good life—that is, a life spent pursuing what is moral, peaceful, fair and just. The contented, happy life is the moral life, in spite of miseries one encounters along the way.

Theologian Ellen Charry suggests that in the modern era happiness became a private matter, an elusive state of mild euphoria pursued through self-fulfillment. Doing good has been pitted against personal happiness.[4] Activities that bring personal enjoyment and pleasure have been put into one box, and activities that bring peace, justice and wisdom have gone into another. The first box we called "happiness" and the second "social obligation," and in the process we have trivialized happiness.

Since happiness now relies on circumstances that are likely to change from moment to moment rather than character qualities that bring a deep sense of satisfaction and well-being, we have the potential to be unhappy more often than not, ever chasing elusive happiness. This other view of happiness—the one held by the ancients—is at the core of mellowness of heart.

WHAT IS A MELLOW HEART?

Mellowness of heart is a way of being that is openly receptive to God so that our lives lean toward a posture of grace, thanksgiving, blessing and goodness. Ronald Rolheiser, Catholic priest and theologian, introduced me to the term in his book *The Holy Longing: The Search for Christian Spirituality*.[5]

Mellowness of heart is captured in the joy expressed by many African Christians. During my daughter Megan's six-month internship in Lilongwe, Malawi, she lived in a place where mellowness of heart abounded. She saw pain, suffering and injustice, yet also joy. Megan wrote:

I have been reflecting on how in a world of cynicism, skepticism, hopelessness, and busyness one of the greatest testimonies to the life that is in Christ is joy. I've come here to experience all of Malawi— every Cherry Plum Soda, every greeting, every hug, every prayer, the small children with wide eyes, the crumbling ceilings, broken down chairs, Madonna t-shirts, morning tea, the many times I choke on the word *injustice* because I have heard myself say it and think it so much and it doesn't come near to doing justice to the injustices around me. But there are also nightly chats with Grace and Grace, when Grace Q. makes a joke and we spend the whole night laughing. All of it—the pain and the joy—this is what I've come for, and it's spectacular, part of the mystery of God's creative hand. Mostly what I find here is joy. I've shared about the pain and suffering I've seen, but this is not my primary experience here. Joy and celebration resound, and strong enough to get me through the questions of poverty, racism and injustice and keep me afloat. I used to live as if the greatest testimony was justice, but one can grow weary and bitter wrestling with the injustices in the world if they do not have joy and thankfulness as their starting point.

Mellowness of heart flows from trusting that we belong not to ourselves but to God, and that we are not entities that stand alone but are part of a whole that connects us to each other and to creation. African Christians do not usually question God in the same way Westerners do. There is greater acceptance of circumstances, both good and bad, and more trust that God is in control of the big picture and will be present with them in their suffering. "I have been made well," they say, releasing to God their pain after sorrowing together, comforting each other and celebrating in the context of community.

Richard Foster describes a fulfillment that comes from losing oneself in a perpetual vision of the Holy. "We are catapulted into something infinitely larger and more real than our petty existence. A blazing God-consciousness frees us from self-consciousness. It is freedom. It is joy. It is life."[6]

As we grow less preoccupied with ourselves, we are filled with wonder at the God who created us and all that surrounds us. We are souls with an identity in God, not autonomous selves, and our life's meaning transcends gratifying ourselves. As we grasp this joyful reality, we become less self-conscious about our successes and failures, our popularity or lack of popularity. We see God in the hard times as well as in the good times. Perhaps we become able to laugh at a human predicament that includes defeat and sorrow, even as we cry.

LAUGHING OUT LOUD

Maintaining deep-seated joy or "happiness" in the midst of despair is unthinkable when happiness depends on favorable circumstances. Mellowness of heart does not require us to deny pain, but it often calls us to look through the darkest circumstances of life to find joy. Sometimes we use humor to express joy; often we use it to express our pain. Sociologists talk about humor as contrasting two different realities—what was expected and what came instead. Humor gives us an alternative to expressing rage or despair as we live in a world never quite measuring up to our expectations.

The role of humor amidst tragedy is perhaps more easily understood through the eyes of an outsider. In the 1961 science-fiction classic *Stranger in a Strange Land* by Robert Heinlein, Mike, a human raised on Mars by peace-loving Martians, is returned to earth as a young man. A quick learner, he soon picks up language and customs, but he struggles with cultural ideas about religion and laughter. It takes him a long time to "get" humor, but he eventually does while watching monkeys in a cage being cruel to each other. Mike says:

> I looked at a cageful of monkeys and suddenly I saw all the mean and cruel and utterly unexplainable things I've seen and heard and read about in the time I've been with my own people—and suddenly it hurt so much I found myself laughing. . . . I had thought—I had been told—that a "funny" thing is a thing of goodness. It isn't. Not ever is it funny to the person it happens to. . . . The goodness is in the laughing itself. I grok [understand] it is a bravery . . . and a sharing . . . against pain and sorrow and defeat.[7]

Humor accepts "wrongness," as Mike calls it, as part of the human predicament. We can curse at wrongness, or we can laugh. Cursing feeds anger and resentment; laughing is bravery, letting go, accepting a world gone awry. When we have mellowness of heart and thus a happiness that transcends our immediate circumstances, our laughter can take on a deeper, richer tone because we know that in the end all will be made right.

So the mellow-hearted laugh—not only in accepting pain but also from the pure delights of seeing a world that is good and beautiful. The soul is well fed through the hearty laughter of friends enjoying each other's company, laughing at the quirky mannerisms that endear us to one another. Humans are drawn to laughter—as we play together, listen to the questions and watch the antics of children, and as we share the stories of our lives.

Receptivity to all of life flows from seeing beauty amidst ashes and holding a picture of hope not yet fulfilled as we partner with God to redeem what has been lost. Mellow-hearted people are paradoxical. They laugh and cry. They see the clouds and the silver linings and in the process see themselves, others and the earth as a flawed creation belonging to a loving and ever-present God. They are joyfully mindful of their obligations to others and to creation, and in their presence we become aware that we too are loved by God.

Mellow-hearted people share God's compassion for the world and desire for *shalom*—a peace represented by justice, not merely the absence of conflict. They hold in tension a humble acceptance of life's hard circumstances and a commitment to working with God for *shalom*.

As a child I loved swinging. It was the closest I could come to satisfying my desire to soar like a bird. Occasionally these days I make my way to the playground at Winfield Elementary School. If the playground is empty, I swing. Working back and forth, I achieve the sweeping arc of childhood in which the taut chains lose their grip for just a second at the highest points of the arc. As I rush toward the sky I tilt back, legs extended, remembering how as a child I'd stretch my toes for the leaves of a tree just beyond my reach. And then I tuck my legs under me as I swing back toward the earth, increasing momentum as I levy my weight forward.

Mellowness of heart requires two separate movements. At times we work to sit with and accept misery, and at times we actively work to eradicate or minimize it.

"GRANT ME THE SERENITY TO ACCEPT THE THINGS I CANNOT CHANGE . . ."

Reinhold Niebuhr, the man most often credited with penning the Serenity Prayer, captured the challenge of the mellow-hearted. We accept what we cannot change, we change what we can, and we seek wisdom to know the difference. Niebuhr then reminds us that God uses hardship to lead us toward peace and that we can trust God will make all things right in the end. In the surrender of our expectations and demands, we will find happiness enough in this life and supreme happiness with God in the next.

My father taught me to look for silver linings in the storm clouds of life's disappointments. Most summers our family spent a week at Spring Canyon, an Officers' Christian Fellowship camp tucked in the mountains of Colorado. One summer Dad, two other men from camp, my brother and I hiked to Mt. Princeton. We drove part of the way up and then still had about a six-hour challenging ascent to the top. As we walked the ridge, snow swooshed up at us from one side of the mountain, swirled above our heads and then fell away from us down the other side. I've never forgotten that, nor the glory of being so high that we were even with other mountain peaks.

We had a long walk back to camp and stopped for lunch in a valley that cradled a lake of melted snow for the refreshment of weary high-altitude mountain climbers. But the eight-hour descent proved more arduous for me than the ascent. After a few hours, every step caused jolting pain in my knees, feet and ankles. I knew my toes were blistered and didn't know if I could make it.

At some point I admitted all this to Dad, in a voice that was trembling and tearful. He said, "When you cry it only makes it harder to breathe. You can do this." He told me to focus on breathing and to think about what a tough and resilient body I had.

Dad always encouraged us to look for hope or to focus on something outside our current troubles to get us through. Today, while I remember the physical pain of that long descent, mostly I remember the glory at the top.

When Dad asked us, "How are you?" we were supposed to say, "Tremendous!" For with God's mercy and grace extended to us, how could anyone be merely "fine"? He was a demanding father, but he lived faithfully, with integrity and deep love and trust in the goodness of God.

Dad found silver linings himself, even when, at sixty-eight, he was diagnosed with a terminal cancer. After radical surgery, radiation and chemo, we all hoped that he had bought at least a couple more good years. But something always emerged to waylay the health we hoped for. He continued to lose weight and developed heart problems, hernias, inexplicable pain in his hips, cataracts in his eyes, hearing loss, and increasing weakness and fatigue.

At one point I asked Dad how he experienced the mounting losses and discomforts of those days. He said, "I think all this pain and trouble is helping me let go of my hold on life. Maybe God knew I needed help with that."

Dad could find silver linings because he believed God loved him and heaven awaited him. The meaning he derived from life transcended his end-of-life circumstances. It came from seeing his connection to something bigger. He died well—without bitterness or anger, maintaining a sense of humor, content with the life God had given him, eventually ready to let go of his hold on earth. Thus Dad died with a mellow heart.

Graciously accepting unhappy circumstances fell out of favor a long time ago. Advances in technology, representative politics and the increasing value placed on individuals have all given us more control of our circumstances and have shaped the way we think about our destiny. Humans, we believe, can and are to be active shapers of their life rather than passive recipients of ill-fated circumstance. The goal is control. So we learn to weed out what makes us unhappy and strengthen our hold on what we think will satisfy.

Our idea of "control" differs from that of the world that existed before the Industrial Revolution. People accepted the limits of a natural world and prayed for daily mercies to cover their needs. "Give us this day our daily bread" has more meaning when bread is not readily available (or affordable) at any number of grocery stores or bakeries. People with limited control over disease, pain, the rhythms of night and day, weather patterns, the cycle of birth, youth, aging and death lived (and still live) with less expectation that they should be able to control the circumstances of their life.

On a backpacking trip in the Chattahoochie Forest of Georgia, my friend Jana and I expected sun. We got rain instead. At the time she was reading *Perelandra*, the second volume in C. S. Lewis's Space trilogy. As we stopped in a shelter with other wayfarers waiting out the rainstorm, she read me the following portion—part of a conversation between Ransom, a human from Earth, and the Lady of Perelandra, a female creature from a world untouched, as yet, by sin. They are talking about our response when we do not get what we hope for—when we even get pain instead. She says:

> What you have made me see is as plain as the sky. . . . One goes into the forest to pick food and already the thought of one fruit rather than another has grown up in one's mind. Then, it may be, one finds a different fruit and not the fruit one thought of. One joy was expected and another is given. But this I had never noticed before—that the very moment of the finding there is in the mind a kind of thrusting back, or setting aside. The picture of the fruit you have *not* found is still, for a moment, before you. And if you wished—if it were possible to wish—you could keep it there. You could send your soul after the good you had expected, instead of turning it to the good you had got. You could refuse the real good;

you could make the real fruit taste insipid by thinking of the other.[8]

Under the shelter Jana and I contemplated the good we got because of the rain. For starters, we heard firsthand the story of the caretakers of the campground where we found shelter. Their families had lived on these mountains for generations—long before the National Park system conceived of stretching a twelve-hundred-mile trail from the Appalachian Mountains in the south through the White Mountains in the north. As we shared stories with other backpackers along the way, we entered a community of hearty souls seeking space and contemplation in nature. We read more, covered less ground and thus observed more intently everything around us. We came looking for one good and received another instead.

As humans learned how to manipulate the physical world, we gained a good measure of control over pain, hunger, disease and aging. The more control we have, the more frustrated and angry we become when we encounter something we can't control. We do not tolerate "misery" well.

The apostle Paul tells us that all things work together for good for those who love God (Rom 8:28), and James admonishes readers to consider trials of every kind a joy because God uses them to test our faith and bring us to maturity (Jas 1:2-4). Too many times I've joined the chorus of those criticizing pious types who toss such verses to people in pain as though to placate hungry dogs with crumbs. "At worst," we say in self-righteousness, "such verses come off sounding like a judgment, at best like a platitude."

Why do I and people like me, who generally have a high regard for Scripture, disregard these passages? Perhaps because we have a worldview that tells us we should fight with all our might to eradicate pain and misery rather than see them as opportunities for developing our character and deepening our faith.

Pain and limits remind us that we are finite, that we depend on the mercies of God for existence, that we can survive hardship and discomfort and grow stronger and deeper through them. These Scriptures speak of a humble acceptance of hardship, reminding us that we have an opportunity to move toward greater maturity. A few verses earlier in Romans 8, Paul tells us that the suffering we now experience is nothing compared to the glory to come. All creation anticipates the day it will be free from death and decay. "For we know that all creation has been groaning as in the pains of childbirth right up to the present time. And even we Christians, although we have the Holy Spirit within us as a foretaste of future glory, also groan to be released from pain and suffering" (Rom 8:22-23).

The wisdom of spiritual mothers and fathers such as Jeremiah Burroughs, a Puritan reformer and preacher of the 1600s, emerged from walking in uncertain and difficult times. Our surest path to contentment, they said, is embracing the goodness of God, even while tempted by our troubles to doubt that God is good at all.

Sometimes I have a hard time believing in some coming glory because all I can see, taste, touch and hear is a dark, bitter and sharp existence. Yet I want to join a creation that groans for redemption. Instead of focusing on the bad God allows and interpreting God's actions as disinterested, unfair or unloving, I can choose to trust that God is all-knowing and is motivated by love for what is good, right and holy. In trusting God, we choose contentment.

The way through our fear is mellowness of heart, a receptivity to all of life. In it we find a gracious willingness to relinquish control, to take that which God sends or allows—not because it is good but because we trust that God works through all things to bring about goodness in the end.

Burroughs did not speak glibly; his times were indeed afflicted. People gave in to addictions, envy, violence and greed. Children died prematurely, as did spouses and parents. Health, and thus the ability to work, was easily lost. Medical insurance and welfare did not catch those who fell ill or into poverty, and gross social injustices were rife in a feudal system where the rich inherited their status and wealth and the peasants their poverty. Yet Burroughs calls Christians to focus on the greatness of God's mercies rather than the littleness of their privileges. [9]

Being content does not mean we are satisfied. In fact, to be content is to know we will always be groaning this side of eternity. Yet when we believe that fullness will come, that there is more than this life, we live with contentment. Mellowness of heart gives us the strength to find joy, even when today disappoints, wounds and is full of injustice.

"COURAGE TO CHANGE THE THINGS I CAN . . ."

Baby lions and tigers make tempting pets. Most people who give in to the temptation to buy one, however, soon find that the responsibility and challenge of feeding and monitoring the behavior of an eight-hundred-pound predatory creature become overwhelming. Most of these pets are euthanized; a few lucky ones make it to Turpentine Creek Wildlife Refuge, a preserve in Arkansas for previously owned wildcats.

As Mark and I toured the refuge, we learned the stories of various animals that had made their way to Turpentine Creek. Sampson and Esmerelda were two magnificent lions raised in cages from infancy until they arrived at Turpentine Creek. When their habitat was ready to receive them, they were given access to a half-acre filled with tall grasses, trees and shrubs. The first day, caretakers opened the door of their lockdown cage so they could run and frolic in the habitat, but Esmerelda and Sampson cowered in their cement facility, too fearful to exit. Caretakers eventually forced them out by turning the water hose on them and then locking them out of their cage for the day. But they hovered near the cage and did not go exploring. Six months later, they had never left their concrete cage to explore the home that awaited them outside.

They seem content with their limited life, preferring the status quo and the predictability of the familiar concrete cage. But their satisfaction is a broken form of contentment that emerges from fear. Some things should be accepted, and some should be challenged and changed.

Mellowness of heart does not excuse brokenness or accept injustice simply because heaven awaits. In swinging, one movement involves stretching out, leaning back and being carried toward the sky. The other involves leaning forward, legs tucked, building momentum as one rushes back toward the earth. Mellowness of heart grows from a commitment to partner with God to work toward healing and *shalom*—to speak truth to and of relationships, social structures, and political, religious and economic institutions. Mellowness of heart is not passive, even if it is a place of grace. It is a platform from which to speak truth to bring healing and justice.

The prophet Jeremiah encouraged exiled Jews in captivity in Babylon to actively move toward *shalom*, even during their long exile. He said:

> "Build homes, and plan to stay. Plant gardens, and eat the food you produce. Marry, and have children. Then find spouses for them, and have many grandchildren. Multiply! Do not dwindle away! And work for the peace and prosperity of Babylon. Pray to the LORD for that city where you are held captive, for if Babylon has peace, so will you."
>
> The LORD Almighty, the God of Israel, says, . . . "The truth is that you will be in Babylon for seventy years. But then I will come and do for you all the good things I have promised, and I will bring you home again. For I know the plans I have for you," says the LORD. "They are plans for good and not for disaster, to give you a future and a hope." (Jer 29:5-11)

Jeremiah told the Israelites that those who put their trust in God are blessed like trees planted along a riverbank, with roots that reach deep into the water, not bothered by the heat or worried by long months of drought (Jer 17). Most of the exiled Jews reading Jeremiah's letter would never return to Israel; the hope they worked toward was for their children and their children's children. Meanwhile they were to strive to create rich and satisfying lives in Babylon.

The Old Testament prophets often spoke out scathing social critiques aimed at those with power and wealth who oppressed the poor, the widow, the orphan and the foreigner. Their words are relevant for today because they spoke of universal sin found in every place and time, and they give us a biblical mandate for pursuing justice against the evil and sin that reside in our social structures and institutions. Prophets denounced their kings and kingdoms because Israel conducted its religious life and ceremonies as God's chosen people yet withheld true worship. At times the nation turned from God toward greed, violence and mistreatment of the powerless.

More than four hundred years later, Jesus also publicly denounced the religious leaders of his day. Pharisees and Sadducees were condemned for false teaching and for perpetuating injustice and lacking mercy even as they kept up public appearances as righteous leaders. Jesus drove merchants and customers out of the temple because they had turned a house of prayer into a den of thieves, a reference to Jeremiah 7:9-11, which the people would have known well:

> Do you really think you can steal, murder, commit adultery, lie, and worship Baal and all those other new gods of yours, and then come here and stand before me in my Temple and chant, "We are safe!"—only to go right back to all those evils again? Do you think this Temple, which honors my name, is a den of thieves? I see all the evil going on there, says the LORD.

Historically prophets had much to lose. As widely unpopular folks, they risked their lives when they spoke out against the status quo and the powerful. Yet Israel (and we) sometimes heeded its prophets and turned from its sin. And because people are capable of changing negative habits and traditions and evaluating and challenging economic and political structures that are harmful, the voice of the prophet, however painfully, brings us hope for redemption.

God has already conquered evil and will ultimately bring this victory to completion and restore *shalom*. We are called to be bold partners with God—sometimes as prophets, sometimes as faithful workers of justice and mercy. Efforts to achieve contentment are incomplete without a struggle for justice. Relinquishing preoccupation with ourselves opens us up to share God's concern for the poor, the disenfranchised, the weak and the downtrodden. This concern and this action characterize a mellow heart.

Mahatma Gandhi exhibited mellowness of heart. He is the man credited with leading a peaceful protest that gave the disinherited of India back their inheritance; he was committed to bringing justice to a country under foreign rule. He believed sorrow and suffering develop character only when they are accepted voluntarily, never when they are imposed. "Action for one's own self binds, action for the sake of others delivers from bondage," he said.[10]

Gandhi shared the life of the poor, wearing their garb, eating simple foods, and using weapons of nonviolence in his efforts with them to throw off British rule and challenge the Indian caste system. Gandhi did not strive for a life characterized by personal peace and contentment, yet he spoke of having a profound contentment. He would say it came from investing his life in seeking justice for the disenfranchised of India.

We don't have to be as renowned as Gandhi to partner with God for *shalom*. Every month *Reader's Digest* prints stories about "everyday heroes." Sometimes they are children, like eleven-year old Pytrce Farmer, a school safety patrol who risked her own life while saving a first-grader who had stepped into traffic.[11] Often they are adults who have saved other children or adults from drowning, fires, muggings or accidents. Occasionally they are whistleblowers like Peter Scannell, who faced personal and financial ruin after exposing one of the biggest mutual-funds scams in history. He is now on disability, is having to dip into savings to live and has been blackballed in the industry. But he said the knowledge that he stood up for the little guy kept him from regret. "I feel very good inside," he says. "You can't put a price on that."[12]

The mellow-heartedness of Debbie and David Alexander is evident in how they opened their home to orphans just after their own children grew up and moved out. They felt called to adopt two boys, orphans from Liberia, after hearing their story during a choir tour to raise money for their orphanage. Over the next couple of years, convinced that families should be together, they adopted the siblings of each boy, who had remained in the orphanage in Liberia, and soon expanded to a household of eight.[13]

We all know women and men who have sacrificed personal goals and dreams to love the world and others as God does. They take on the care of an aging parent or a high-needs child, or they sponsor a refugee family. Some volunteer in prison ministry, mentor high-risk youth, or help pregnant teens and new single parents. All these actions, whether large-scale or small, one-time acts or lifetime commitments, pull our lives and our world toward redemption. We extend mercy and pursue justice.

When I am in the presence of mellow-hearted souls, I am comforted and calmed. I respect and seek out their wisdom. They are truth tellers, speaking of what they observe and conclude, not what they know I most want to hear. Their lives are characterized by concern for others that comes from seeing people through the eyes of God. They laugh and play, give and receive, work and rest, and embrace life and others even while speaking truth. I am at ease in their presence, though sometimes rightly challenged to think carefully about how I live. In their presence I am encouraged to step beyond the safety of the familiar to explore the wild and wondrous beyond the concrete walls of my comfortable existence.

"AND WISDOM TO KNOW THE DIFFERENCE"

Since mellowness of heart includes both a gracious acceptance of life's circumstances and a willingness to fight circumstances that are unjust, we need wisdom to know when to accept circumstances and when to fight to change them. Themes of Scripture, religious traditions as lived out through the ages, and the examples of godly and wise people help illuminate the way.

If the change we want to bring is to provide shalom *for someone else, then it is likely good.* God's prophets defended widows, orphans, foreigners and the poor; Gandhi's life mission was to change political and social structures to better the lives of India's outcasts; the rescuers and caretakers at Turpentine Creek provide care to some of God's abused creatures. We have many testimonies of the importance of challenging the status quo, of actively working to bring healing and justice. Bringing peace and justice to others is good. We may disagree on whether or not gun control is a social good or how peace should be pursued in the Middle East, but we are all called to work toward *shalom,* to get informed, to vote responsibly and to act.

If change will provide shalom *for us personally, it still may be good.* We need to avoid both fatalism that paralyzes any action on our own behalf and a tendency to do all we can to eradicate personal misery by controlling our destiny and bettering our life. Jesus commended and healed those who asked for it. He stopped the bleeding of the hemorrhaging woman, made a paralytic walk, blind men see and lepers clean. Martin Luther King Jr. worked for justice that would benefit himself and his children, as well as the southern African Americans he represented. When we seek help for physical ailments or clinical depression, for guidance about finances, career calling or relationships, we are recognizing our need for healing and wholeness and God's desire to redeem and restore that which is broken and distorted. Pursuing this kind of change moves us toward others, toward community and toward *shalom*.

Sometimes circumstances can be changed, but acceptance may be a better good. Many of the changes we pursue are about bringing us a greater sense of control over our life or perceived happiness. We seek a better church, job, home, partner, and fail to see the value of staying put, accepting what is, growing our character through disappointment, deepening our knowledge through patience and forbearance. God redeems pain, struggle and various forms of self-defined misery by using them to shape and strengthen our character, to draw us toward God and to remind us that we are not in control. Sometimes sitting with our sadness, rather than moving too quickly to eradicate it, brings a deeper understanding of this broken world and God's movement in it. When we groan with all creation for redemption, we are acknowledging that we will never be satisfied this side of eternity. We learn to find contentment in the good we have. So we find meaningful relationships in our imperfect churches, unexpected friendliness in our neighbors, greater satisfaction in jobs where we think we are not adequately appreciated, and love from friends, roommates and spouses whom we also fail to love perfectly.

If circumstances can't be changed, then acceptance is the pathway to peace. Sometimes no amount of fighting will change our circumstances, and fighting only keeps us from discovering the good God will bring from the bad we are experiencing. In 1967 seventeen-year-old Joni Eareckson took a dive on a summer day and became a quadriplegic for life. In *The God I Love: A Lifetime of Walking with Jesus*, Joni Eareckson Tada tells her story as a woman who drifted from God, returned to God and continued throughout her life to struggle with times of depression. She said she learned that there are more important things in life than walking.[14] As she accepted her paralysis, she moved ahead to become an artist— painting with a brush between her teeth—a writer, speaker, and the founder of Joni & Friends, an organization that helps other disabled people. Joni is a mellow-hearted soul, one willing to accept the suffering God allowed to define her life.

Our society offers medical technologies that give us a fair amount of control, or perceived control, over our health. When faced with our mortality, a handicap, losses that come from living in a physical body that ages and decays, it is difficult to choose to let go of control. The cost of hanging on to youth or life, hanging on to the sadness of losing a child, spouse, friend, hanging on to the bitterness of losing a job or a dream is high. When we choose to accept loss, we gain something altogether different. We hold life and others loosely, relinquishing the burden of being in control, and look instead for the small wonders, the tender mercies that help us find peace along the way toward eternity. We seek consolation in our connection to a bigger picture, a transcendent reality, as we remember we are souls that belong to God. In the process, we exercise mellowness of heart.

"AND SUPREMELY HAPPY WITH HIM FOREVER IN THE NEXT"
In premodern days, knowledge was assumed to exist outside individuals. Those seeking knowledge "thirsted and hungered" after it, believing they needed to be receptive learners who grasped reality because it called to them. So they studied and learned the movement of stars and planets, the healing power of herbs, the habits and patterns of animals. They did not believe that they *created* knowledge or that it resided within them, but that they were grasping an existing knowledge that existed outside of them. Theology professor A. J. Conyers summarizes a difference between a modern and premodern concept of knowledge when he says that in the premodern mind, "ideas were not true because they captured the imagination, but they captured the imagination because they were true."[15]

Given our inclination to be autonomous selves who find our own truth and make our own way toward happiness, our unhappiness may well bubble up from a definition of happiness that depends on circumstances. The belief that we must find ourselves and create our own truth makes it difficult to relinquish what is, after all, a false perception of how much control we have over our existence. An alternative, premodern view suggests that life's meaning exists outside of us. Christian theology tells us that happiness comes from embracing a God-centered life rooted in the atoning work of Jesus.

A mellow heart lets go of the need for control and looks for the good that might come to us from the unexpected. This is easier when we are confident that our supreme happiness will come in eternity. As the mellow-hearted relinquish control over their own destiny, they become ever more preoccupied with the goodness and mercy of God, eagerly looking to partner with God to bring mercy and justice to others. And so we move between acceptance of some misery and rejection of other misery, praying for wisdom to know what to accept and what to reject.

Mellowness of heart cannot be achieved by directly pursuing it, any more than contentment can be purchased from a real estate agent, a travel agent or a yoga instructor. Mellowness of heart comes from learning to yield one's preoccupation with self in favor of a vision of the goodness of God and one's soul as part of an interconnected whole held in the hands of God. Then we can better embrace what God allows, even when it is that which we most want to avoid.

QUERIES FOR FURTHER REFLECTION

- How have you willingly accepted some hardship? What redemptive outcome did it have in your life?

- Jeremiah talked about building homes, planting gardens and praying for the prosperity of Babylon during Israel's captivity. How is the message of Jeremiah relevant for you? What silver lining might be present in a circumstance you are currently experiencing that brings you discomfort, pain or distress?

- Where have you tried to escape distress and perhaps missed an opportunity for spiritual or personal growth?

- Jesus accused the religious leaders of his day of entirely missing the point of true worship. How is your church vulnerable to missing the point, to going through the motions of religion without caring for the poor, the widow, the orphan, the foreigner? What can you do about it?

- If you were to submit an "Everyday Heroes" piece to *Reader's Digest*, what story would you tell? Who among your friends or family members has been an everyday hero?

- Exercise: This week, take a step in working with God to redeem some piece of the broken world around you, in your home, neighborhood or community, church, the world.

EMBRACING LIMITS

The secret to happiness is not in getting more but in wanting less.

ELAINE ST. JAMES

We packed up our Toyota—food staples, my espresso maker, a picnic lunch, clothes (mostly of the jeans and T-shirts variety), camera, binoculars, flashlight and aging laptop computers. With another academic year finished, Mark and I were leaving the suburbs of Chicago for a cabin ten miles outside of Eureka Springs, Arkansas. We had scheduled this week away to rest and gear up for summer writing.

Coming off a particularly full semester of teaching, I needed some space before engaging in any reflective writing, so I spent quiet mornings sitting on the balcony, sipping coffee and watching eagles soar over the valley. One morning I hiked down to Beaver Lake. Much of the path consisted of rocky slate, and I found what I hoped was an arrowhead laying on the edge of the path. But after learning from a local that my eagles were turkey vultures, I doubted that my rock was an arrowhead. Always an optimist, though, I decided to take it home to an anthropologist colleague who studies the Mayan Indians. He would know if what I held was slate that had been chipped and broken by wind, rain and the tumbling of rock against rock, or by the people who called these mountains home long before developers thought to build glass-front cabins that looked over the valley and Beaver Lake.

My life is significantly different from the lives of those who lived here before. The arrowhead reminds me that I have fewer limits on my life than the early inhabitants of this place did. I don't hunt my food and do not have to rely only on fruits, nuts and vegetables I can gather or grow in my neighborhood. My house can be heated or cooled with electricity and gas. We can drive, fly or take a train when we want to travel. Surgery (or therapy) can fix or replace our ailing hearts, and vaccines protect us from debilitating diseases. The unlimited life encourages me to push back limits and to value, expect and seek increasing comfort and ease. We're not particularly good at accepting limits, particularly if comfort is involved.

I also became aware of a strong sense of community connections and history. As I walked the garden paths surrounding Blue Springs—for many centuries a gathering place for native people—and later along the streets of Eureka Springs, I could feel the history, the power of deep connections forged in these mountains. Some current residents' families have lived here for generations, catering to the hordes of vacationers drawn to this place over the years. My own home is in a rather transient community alongside others who have left roots elsewhere to pursue opportunities in the Midwest. Nearly all of my colleagues at Wheaton College are transplants as I am, trying to put down roots or planning a retirement that will return us to a place we still call "home." Many of us long for connections in our highly mobile, on-the-move lives.

I have to carve out time to sip and savor life. For the most part, renewal and reflection are not built into my modern life and its daily routines. This was a third difference I observed between my life and the lives of those who lived in Arkansas long before our government bought it as part of the Louisiana Purchase: reflection, rest, various kinds of work, and celebration with kin and community were a normal part of life. An-thropologists tell us that contrary to popular belief, hunting and gather-ing cultures probably had plenty of time for what we call "leisure." Many of these groups had a rich verbal culture and a complex kinship net-work, where nights around the fire were times of community and shar-ing.[1] Time to reflect, rest and celebrate with kin and community de-creased as lives became increasingly characterized by distinct social classes wedded to the economic system of emerging nation-states. Peas-ants in feudal systems worked very hard and long hours, with little time for leisure. They were a powerless underclass, easily exploited and op-pressed. Today the working poor around the world still work long hours or at multiple jobs in an effort to eke out a livable wage.

For reasons related to choice rather than need or oppression, time to reflect, rest and connect with family and friends is also minimal for the middle and upper classes. Those who feel pressure to make the most of every opportunity often end up living frenetic lives trying to secure the American Dream, taking care of possessions and acquisitions, filling calendars and driving or flying here and there for the activities and en-gagements that are expected and available for those with middle- or upper-class standing.

Except for the working poor, who have less choice in the matter, re-newal, reflection and restful time with kin have to be chosen, intention-ally planned for and sought, and Eureka Springs draws tent campers and resort residents alike who are pursuing these blessings. Some come seek-ing solitude and a quiet place to fish. Others take advantage of places like the New Moon Spa and the one-hundred-plus-year-old Palace Bath House, which offer mineral water baths, eucalyptus steam barrels and modern-day massage—remnants of the days when world travelers came to these medicinal springs for healing and renewal. Sipping and savoring life is easier out here. Reconnection with peace and a future hope emerges when I take time to reflect on my life, my place in the world, the gifts of this good earth and the God who sustains it.

A significant difference between those who lived in the Ozark Mountains before white settlers showed up and the settlers' progeny, who hunt for arrowheads instead of game, is that the former lived more comfortably within the limits of their physical existence. Native people tended to see themselves as part of the earth that sustained them, neither set apart from it nor master over it. The young learned the skills of drawing sustenance and healing from the earth in a way that respected the created world and its creatures. They drew from the earth what they needed, but rarely more, teaching their young a sustainable existence that was perpetuated throughout most of human history.

Contented people I have observed, read about and talked with live with different expectations from those most of us cherish. They accept more limits. Many have a strong sense of belonging and being part of something bigger than themselves, so they craft a life built on a future hope. They seek rest, renewal and reflection so they can continue to find joy in being with, serving and working alongside others. It is as though they stepped aside a moment, observed a discontented and disconnected world, and then discovered a signpost leading down another path.

I am not a naysayer of progress, and this is not a call back to some idyllic earlier life. Every era has had its share of troubles and tribulations. Some stole what did not belong to them and took advantage of or abused other people, creatures and the creation that sustained them, doing more harm than good with their lives. But every era has also been gifted with those who lived graciously, generously and gently, leaving behind a legacy of blessing. I want to learn how to live wisely and well in my circumstance, as they did in theirs.

So I do not eschew progress. I admire Wendell Berry, the farmer-poet-philosopher who writes with a pencil and paper, but I unapologetically use a computer. I take advantage of the technology that makes it easy to communicate with my mother in Pennsylvania, my daughters during their three- and six-month stays in Peru, Honduras and Malawi, and my advisees—students on internships in developing countries around the world. I have benefited from antibiotics, refrigerators, the free press and the right to vote.

Progress, we decided collectively, is good. Progress has increased the complexity of our lives and given us more choices and opportunities, but it has also diminished our obligations to and dependency on others. We trusted it to bring us the Good Life, but progress was expensive. We made a down payment and are now realizing how much we've been paying in interest charges over the last generation or two. My hope is to find a way through the choices before me to the Good Life modeled by Jesus and illuminated in Scripture. I want to rediscover places of the renewal, reflection and connection I lost sight of as I seek contentment in a complex era that is rich in opportunity.

THE REALITIES OF EARTHY LIVING

God gave us earthy bodies, that is, bodies of the earth that are amazingly strong and resilient. But having earthy bodies subject to natural laws means we bump up against physical limits. We can't grow cantaloupe in our backyard in the winter, see well in the dark, cure all our ailments or resist growing old. We cannot eat, drink or inhale any substance we want without consequence, nor function optimally on four hours of sleep. We have limits. We are frail.

As humans endowed with the capacity to create, we have always worked to push back limits—to have more daylight, mobility, a longer youth and fewer consequences for our unwise but enticing choices. Many of our inventions have been geared at freeing us from the limits of our frailty.

Aging is one of the earthy limits we confront if we are fortunate enough to grow old. Keeping our body active, feeding it well, resting adequately and pursuing healthy habits honor God by showing respect for the good gift of our body. Besides, they extend the good use we can get from our aging body. Odile Atthalin, a vibrant and active sixty-eight-year-old woman, chooses to age naturally rather than to have cosmetic surgery. When people see her dance or watch her from a distance, they assume she is much younger. She likes challenging how people think about what it means to be old; instead of changing her face, Atthalin would like to change the way people perceive aging. She says, "I've seen very old people extremely energetic and beautiful. Like oozing a glow. A deep inner contentment. That's why I know it is possible, and that's how I know it's what I want. If I have the glow, I don't care how many wrinkles I have."[2]

I have crow's feet emerging around my eyes and puckering skin around my lips. I want to see them as signs that I have experienced a life filled with grace—that I have smiled, laughed, thought hard, slept well, worked, cried and kissed. My hope is that the passing of years as etched on my body will be a testimony that I have sought to live with intention, mindful of Jesus as my model for how to live and love well, and aware of the presence of God's Spirit to help, comfort and guide. So I'm holding out against my birth cohort, the group currently feeling the most pressure to spend money to cling to youthful appearance. I don't expect that holding out will get me the respect granted our aging ancestors; there are not yet enough Odile Atthalins among us. But every holdout contributes one more voice that stands against the pressure to exalt youthfulness as the symbol of value, power and success. And as Odile has a glow, I have a peace that comes from accepting the limits imposed by my aging body, and I am released from the expectation to control something I cannot ultimately control. Instead I choose to celebrate each birthday, a marker that I've been granted one more year to grow wiser, to continue to learn how to live well, content and at peace with myself, others and God.

Fatigue is another physical limit that we can accept by ceasing our activity or fight with No-Doz or other caffeine-laden products that alter our physical state and push back limits. Some days I feel utterly spent as I strive to satisfy unusual demands and high expectations. At the end of such a day, my weary body calls me toward the solitude and rest of a soak in the tub followed by an early bedtime. Sometimes I listen and slide into a tub of water, letting the warmth of water soothe away the tension of the day. I am accepting the limits of my body, accepting fatigue as a reminder of the frailty of my humanity and enjoying the rest that comes from releasing the need to overcome and control my human limitations. This is decidedly easier to do now that our children are grown. But even when they were young, Mark would take them for a walk or outside to play on days when an hour of evening solitude was the best gift he could offer. How hard it must be for single parents who do not have the luxury of accepting the limits of fatigue! May we be Christ to each other—those of us with an abundance of rest finding ways to offer some as a gift to those for whom rest is a scarcity.

When we allow ourselves to nap when we are weary, to stay home when we are ill, to be less productive than is possible, we are respecting our human limitations. We relinquish the need to constantly push to have or do more, or to keep up, and instead welcome opportunities to slow down, to rest. Accepting physical limits allows us to relish fruits in their season—literally and figuratively.

When we live with physical limits, we are more likely to have a deep and even sacred appreciation for what is finite. Feasts were more meaningful for those who depended on the fall harvest for food that would sustain them through the winter and spring. Today most of us could put together a Thanksgiving feast as easily in the spring as in the fall—the pumpkin, turkey, potatoes, cranberries, green beans, squash and apples are available and plentiful year round. We have no seasons of scarcity from which we emerge with thankful hearts for the bounty of the harvest. Unless we choose them. Some do this by purchasing only fruits and vegetables grown locally and in season, savoring the glorious weeks when berries, peaches and corn are at their peak. They don't take the bursting flavors of summer and fall for granted—produce that tastes richer, in fact, because it is picked ripe and eaten shortly thereafter, rather than picked (sometimes early), treated and shipped across the country, continent or ocean.

We gain a stronger appreciation that we are finite when we fast from what we take for granted. The invitation to fast, like observing the sabbath, is an ancient spiritual discipline that reminds us we are dependent on God, who sustains life. Occasionally I enter a season of fasting in which once a week I refrain from eating until the evening meal. I emerge from my fasts thankful for food and most hungry for simple foods like good bread, fresh steamed vegetables, fruit. I want to emerge from fasting mindful of and prayerful for children and adults around the world who go to bed hungry at night through no choice of their own. But fasting is uncomfortable physically, and it reminds me of uncomfortable realities about hunger in the world, and for these reasons I am reluctant to do it. I want to learn to sit with this physical and spiritual discomfort— and to grow deeper in my love and more mindful.

Those I talked with or read about who intentionally accept physical limits sometimes spoke of it as a moral choice that came from recognizing that they are to live in partnership with the created world, not as conquerors of it. Others talked of how accepting physical limits has been good for their soul and for their community. So they are cautious about which limit-busting innovations they welcome. Members of intentional communities, writer-farmers like Wendell Berry and other individuals living with limits carefully take from the earth, seeking to minimize their use of the world's gifts and resources that others may flourish.

WANTING AND CHOOSING LESS

Progress pushed back the limits of a physical existence we considered unnecessarily harsh and primitive and gave us a life of greater ease. We grow up believing that hardworking people will be rewarded with money enough to buy ease and more happiness—nice homes, nice vacations, the newest time-saving gadgets, age-defying cosmetic treatments. We don't actually have to wait until we've earned the money either. What we can't pay for today we are encouraged to pay for tomorrow using credit. We want to be happy and are encouraged to believe these purchases will quiet the discontent that rumbles around in our soul. We may mute the rumble, but it doesn't go away. The secret to happiness, says Elaine St. James, is not getting more but wanting less. When we limit our consumption, we learn to enjoy what is simple, and in consuming less we remind ourselves of what brings contentment.

I have pleasant memories of a 1960s childhood, memories that were made possible because of the limits of the day. My three siblings and I took turns washing dinner dishes. We had a washer, a dryer and a putter-awayer. The fourth sibling had the night off. We rotated the jobs, keeping track easily enough. I liked washing best; the texture of suds on plates and silverware felt pleasing to my fingers. I tried to stay ahead of the dryer and to finish far ahead of the putter-awayer and thus win in some private competition. We accepted dishwashing as a job that needed doing, and I think we did it graciously enough—though memory fails me on some of these details! When I asked my mother, she said that most of the time we had a dishwasher—so these pictures linger from brief periods in childhood when we did not. Working together with my siblings, standing at the sink with my brother on a chair because he was too short to help otherwise, is a precious and nostalgic memory.

I also remember raking and burning Oregon leaves with my family in the fall. Using our bodies and working together brought a kind of soothing togetherness—I belonged and contributed, part of something bigger than myself. I remember cooling off one humid summer we spent in Florida before central air conditioning. My brother and I would lie side by side and take turns getting right in front of the fan, speaking "ahhhh" into the blades and catching the chopped-up sound as it blew back in our face. And I remember coasting down a steep hill after pedaling hard to the top—and pretending I was flying. I have many memories of the simple play and work that filled my days, forged a place of belonging in my family and brought my soul contentment.

Over time, both simple pleasures and arduous tasks were replaced with bigger and better things we could buy to ease the "hardship" of living. Central air conditioning and dishwashers came alongside clothes dryers, snowblowers, microwaves, video games and Disneyland vacations. In the name of carefree entertaining, we used paper plates, plastic forks, spoons and cups, and paper napkins. The modern life increasingly brought us disposable, instant and easy products that we adopted without noticing that doing so altered our family and community relationships and changed the way we thought about resources, free time and work. "Resources" became the money we had available to spend, instead of the electricity, petroleum products, water, lumber or clean air we were consuming. "Free time" became time I had freed up with my resources to use as I wanted—watching TV, golfing, shopping. "Work" became the opposite of free time and something to grumble about having to do to get enough resources to purchase the Good Life. We easily lose sight of an integrated life that includes various activities we do as we provide for and grow our family, celebrate with and invest in our community, living so as to make the world a better place.

Wanting and choosing less helps us live more integrated and content lives. Berry refuses to own a computer or a television,[3] uses horses to plow his fields, and writes with a pen and paper. He is a conservationist in that he wants to avoid the extravagant use of electricity that has a long history of ravaging the Appalachian Mountains for coal; he wants to make use of simple tools and techniques as he goes about the business of living. He doesn't believe that he would gain anything worth the cost to the earth or his family and community relationships by wanting and choosing more, especially technology intended to give him more control or more "free time."

Bob McIntosh, the husband of my mother-in-law, inspired me to return to a simple practice I had kept throughout the early years of my marriage. Bob does his household's laundry, and he hangs clothes outside to dry. I didn't think anyone did that anymore. I didn't even know if one could buy a clothesline anywhere. But a couple of years ago I went looking and found a place online where I could purchase an umbrella clothesline. I ordered it, Mark set the pole in concrete, and I began hanging out our laundry. Hanging laundry gives me an excuse to be outside, grants me some satisfaction that I am not burning fossil fuels to do what the sun can do effortlessly, and allows Mark and me the simple pleasure of slipping into a bed with sheets smelling of sun and air. Plus I've had the joy of watching two neighboring households string up lines of their own and occasionally join me in the hanging of laundry. We're starting a neighborhood revolution.

The Amish in the United States serve as an example of a community of people who are very intentional about which technologies they accept and which they reject. They have sustained their way of life for almost three hundred years by maintaining some separation from a culture eager to adopt new technologies. Each innovation is carefully evaluated before it's adopted, and they limit technology most of us welcome unless it will help keep their lives simple and their families intact. They believe that most of what we embrace for the sake of greater ease weakens the strength of community bonds, increasingly isolating people from each other by diminishing their need for each other.

Not all current day agricultural-based communities are Amish. The forty-three Christian families who make up the Homestead Heritage include a philosophy professor, physician, lawyer and insurance adjustor. Heritage homesteaders are intentional about wanting and choosing less, accepting limits associated with their simple existence. The families live on a 510-acre farming community in Texas, where they break their fields with horse-drawn plows, raise pasture-fed beef free of antibiotics and hormones, farm organically, offer classes and homemade products to the public, and homeschool their children. Their babies tend to be born at home, and their elderly usually die at home. They make their own clothes, grow their food and build their barns and houses. Outsiders are welcome to participate in their festivals, buy their products, take their craft courses and seminars—all of which can be explored through their webpage.[4] The homesteaders are avid readers and prolific writers, and they share a corporate sense of responsibility for and accountability to the group. In return for the limits they accept, they receive various blessings that come as unexpected surprises that nurture their souls.

One blessing from limiting our consumption comes from rediscovering our treasures: old or used, passed down and already ours. When we relinquish the need to obtain the "new and improved," we can appreciate the good we have. I am wrapped in a sense of story and tradition every Saturday when I wind the mantel clock my mother gave me for my forty-seventh birthday. It is more than one hundred years old and belonged to my father's grandparents. It makes a soothing tick-tock sound, marks the hours and half-hours with a full deep chime and still keeps very good time. Whenever we pull out our twenty-eight-year-old KitchenAid mixer or the shovel, pitchfork, hoe or hammer we inherited from Mark's grandfather, we are acknowledging the workmanship of old, well-crafted tools that do not need replacing. When I wear my grandmother's wedding ring I remember, throughout the day, the women from whom I have come. On lightly rainy Chicago days when I wear the George Fox College soccer jacket I bought used almost twenty years ago, when the team replaced its uniforms, I am reminded of our George Fox friends and my Oregon and Quaker roots.

Other people's old castoffs can acquire new stories, along with a secondhand life, like the chair I now have in my office. About ten years ago Mark, our dog Chale and I were out walking in our suburban neighborhood. It was the eve of garbage collection day, and people had put out their cans, bins and household discards by the curb. At one curb, sitting beside a large garbage can, was a wooden chair, its seat cushion covered with yellow plastic, its white paint chipping and cracked, evidence of weather damage. I saw it as a treasure; Mark was certain it was trash. But he graciously accepts my efforts to redeem treasure from trash, so he did little to dissuade me. Still, uncertain of the legality of my intentions or the desirability of the chair, he agreed to take Chale and head home. I flipped the chair over, hoisted it onto my head and carried it to redemption.

Sure enough, from beneath the white paint emerged a beautiful oak chair, slightly damaged by exposure to rain and sun, but stately and strong. I replaced the yellow plastic with a rich fabric and have used the chair in my office at work ever since.

I like that my chair was redeemed from trash. It reminds me that I am ever being crafted into a story that adds another bit to the tale of humanity, and that my life needs redemption from the errors and arrogance of my thinking and choices. When we relish what is old, used, passed down or already ours, we are less tempted by the market-driven consumerism that would send us on a never-ending quest to figure out the good we don't have and to somehow obtain it.

A second blessing comes from an appreciation for what is finite. Such an appreciation honors our connection to the earth that sustains us and often leads to creative and innovative ways of reusing and consuming fewer resources. My grandmother regularly went through the laundry and pulled out socks that needed darning. She darned socks only once each, but she darned them early and well. She also adjusted hems and seams for her children's growing bodies and handed down clothes from one child to the next. My mother also did this. When Grandma sent us three matching blue plaid dresses, as the youngest I wore my dress until I grew out of it, then I wore Kathy's, who was wearing Pamela's. I spent four or five years wearing beautiful blue plaid dresses stitched by my grandmother while she held me in mind. Grandma made dishtowels from the muslin sacks that had held the flour she purchased from the grocer. Food scraps were fed to farm animals or composted. Milk came from the cows on the farm, and those who bought it received it in glass jugs that were returned empty to be filled again.

Grandma had a lot less trash than I do, and none of it was plastic. She had less garbage partly because merchants and consumers alike used less paper, less packaging, less of everything. Grandma, like most women of her generation, found creative uses for paper bags, socks that could no longer be darned, stockings with runs in them, cardboard, muslin sacks, even the three-pound tin cans that had held her coffee beans. For Grandma, this economy of resources was a taken-for-granted way of life.

I have to be intentional about using less, buying less, fixing (rather than replacing) broken things and reusing what I would usually discard. In the United States we have abundance at our fingertips. Drawing on our country's resources, as well as on resources around the world, we have grown accustomed to taking advantage of what is available. People in the United States use almost 120 pounds of natural resources per person each day to support our lifestyle. That's twice as much as Germans, 12 times more than Chinese and 114 times more than people from Bangladesh.[5] We leave a large footprint as we walk the earth.

When I limit what I use, I become mindful of and thankful for God's created world. I am a partner of the earth and give to it even as I take from it. I give by learning the place I live—what plants grow well where. I feed and water the birds and butterflies with bird baths and feeders and by planting what nurtures them. As I grow my tomatoes, onions, peppers, zucchini and cucumbers in the small raised beds in my backyard, I am mindful of the good dirt that gives me food—and the oxygen, sunshine and water that grow it. In this way I feel the rhythm of the creation from which I came and honor the harmony intended between living things. When we learn to step lightly on the earth that sustains us, we are more likely to give attention, praise and care as we take from it what we need to live.

When we limit our consumption, we remind ourselves that we too are finite. And seeing ourselves as we are—vulnerable, frail, always desiring more—allows us to admit our need for others, our need for God, our insatiable longings ("we are Grand Canyons without a bottom," as Ronald Rolheiser says[6]), and to join a community life that strengthens, sustains and nurtures us as we live on earth, anticipating heaven.

LIMITING OUR DRIVE FOR SELF-DETERMINATION

Choices reflect values. Values determine whether we go away to pursue career opportunities elsewhere or stay and work near family and kin. We hold values about cohabiting, attending church, buying American and being self-determining people who make our way in the world.

At several points in the last one hundred years, the Western value of self-determination has led subcultures, sometimes countercultures and more recently pop culture to so emphasize self-empowerment that all laws and authority structures were approached with grave suspicion. A couple of years ago, "DEFY" was the advertisement theme for an athletic shoe. In a thirty-second commercial cutting rapidly from images to printed words, viewers see a progression of Things to Defy. We see an adolescent boy defying gravity: with these shoes, the image suggested, you can run up and over parked cars and spike a volleyball into the face of your opponent. An adolescent smashes a pie in the face of a man in a business suit. We see quick hints of illicit sex. The back doors of an animal-control vehicle are opened by an adolescent, releasing a pack of dogs. A man escapes the police, another his execution. All these acts defy authority and in the process reinforce certain values:

freedom from limitations, from obligation, from authority; freedom to be self-determining.

"Manifest destiny" was the belief that those who came to settle the United States were intended by God to explore and conquer North America, ultimately creating a nation that would usher in God's kingdom on earth. When we ran into interference, such as native people and their ideas about the sacredness of land and land ownership, we excused breaking treaties with them. They were seen as savages or childlike innocents who didn't understand progress, freedom or manifest destiny.

So we marched forward and claimed our territory—intent on building a country of self-determining people. Yet a groundswell of people are revisiting values depicted by a self-determination that defies authority, or the mandate to pursue self-fulfillment—"Just Do It," "You Deserve It"— and the credit card companies that say, "It's Everywhere You Want to Be" and "Don't Leave Home Without It." They are recognizing contentment comes from embracing values that help them recognize their connections and necessary dependence on others, and obligations to them, freeing them to accept some limits, and to craft a life that allows for rest, renewal and reflection.

Some of the limits we choose to accept or reject are moral ones. Generally if we steal, commit adultery or murder, we know we are breaching a moral limit. Most people acknowledge laws regarding morality as good and necessary—the moral life is indeed the good life. God imposed certain limits out of a desire for goodness, for our sake and the sake of creation. God placed a limit on Adam and Eve, abundantly giving them access to all the fruits and vegetables in the Garden of Eden except for one tree. The limit was a reminder to them, and subsequently to all of us, that we are not God but bearers of God's image, created to be in fellowship with God and other humans and to live harmoniously with creation. Limiting our drive for self-determination brings with it both expected and unexpected goods.

One good associated with limiting our self-determination is freedom and contentment gained from relinquishing the need to control others and our circumstances. Living with limits takes us back to our dependence on God and reminds us that we are not, in fact, in control. This truth is very liberating. When we relinquish control, we accept limitations. We become willing to submit to the authority and counsel of elders who have lived long and gained wisdom along the way, even if imperfect wisdom. Jesus didn't come to arrange the world so that it matched his picture of ideal (and his picture would have been truly ideal!). We will find greater peace if we relinquish our tendency to control. Lowering our expectations that colleagues, friends, children and spouses share our picture of what makes for a perfect gathering, vacation, workplace environment, friendship or family life will make us more gracious, warm and welcoming—more like Jesus.

When we relinquish the need for control, we are not driven to adopt the latest product or technology that promises to give us more energy, more productive time or a more perfect life. In this acceptance we are liberated from the pressure to earn more, produce more, do more, orchestrate perfection. We become free to live more gentle lives.

A second good of accepting limits on our self-determination is related to relinquishing control—it is giving up the drive for personal perfection. The fact that something can be done better doesn't mean it *has* to be. When we graciously accept the messiness of imperfect people with imperfect lives (including our own), we receive blessing, and we bless those around us. Jesus accepted people as they were, meeting them in their messiness, imperfection and even wrongheadedness.

Tim and Val, our longtime friends in Oregon, had a home that always welcomed friends. Not because they kept dust off their furniture and clutter in the closet (I have no memory of this either way) but because they welcomed you as family, not as company. They were kind and gracious, and their hospitality was not encumbered by a drive for perfection. A number of years ago we were back in Oregon for Christmas and visited them the day before our scheduled return to Illinois. We reminisced about the annual New Year's Eve party they used to host before we and other friends moved away in search of other dreams (they were the only ones who had returned). In half an hour we were scrambling to recreate one—they called our mutual friends from Seattle to come home for the day, we arranged to postpone our flight, and we put together food from Val's well-stocked pantry. Because there was no expectation for perfection, we pulled off a grand reunion of friends and memories, our children playing together as they had in years past while we adults played games, laughed and remembered our bond of friendship. In the early morning hours, we gathered our sleeping children from the living-room floor and made our way to the airport, our hearts full and warm.

In the presence of people who are not driven to achieve perfection, we do not worry whether our clothes are quite right or what they will think of us if our children are behaving badly or if we have added poundage to our frame. They allow us to relax in the messiness of a world that, for most people, includes dust, grease spots, wrinkles, noisy children, quick-serve meals and weight fluctuations. When we stop striving for perfection, we become more gracious to ourselves and more gracious to those who live with us, work with us or call us friends.

CREATIVE POSSIBILITIES

As humans endowed with the capacity to create, we reflect God's nature in our art and architecture, our gardening design and music composition, our tools and machines. Some of our creative energy has always been directed at pushing back limits—to have more choices, to have a more abundant life. Desires for choice, wealth and freedom to determine our own lives drove the inventions that have brought us greater ease, freedom from constraints and unprecedented abundance. Limits were minimized, and life was filled to the brim. People lived longer, healthier lives; fewer died prematurely of disease. We engineered and constructed physical structures and political and economic systems, and in the creating, we reflected a creative energy infused in us by our Creator.

Progress is not all good nor all bad. Neither is it neutral. The things we invent are based on values we hold and assumptions we make. Some of those values and assumptions are shortsighted. That we have not limited our use of resources because we believe the earth can indefinitely supply us with goods is a wrongheaded assumption. Most biologists studying the environment agree that we are overusing resources and significantly damaging every aspect of our biosphere and the life sustained by it.[7] Living sustainable lives means we clarify the difference between artificially created *wants* and real *needs*. We would be wise to heed the critiques of knowledgeable people who lived before us, the native people who continue to challenge our assumptions about how we subdue and rule the earth, and those in the biological and environmental sciences who are sounding the alarm for this generation. They call us to live sustainable lives that take from the earth only what is needed and give back in kind to preserve the earth's beauty and gifts for generations to come.

The wise throughout history have always believed that contentment comes not from having more things but from wanting the right things. Progress, as defined by new and improved technology that provides greater ease and prosperity and pushes back the limits of our frail humanity, will not satisfy the yearning of our hearts. We need to learn, or perhaps just remember, how to pursue the right things, to want the Good Life as described throughout Scripture—connection to others, justice, peace, hope and love, beautiful aspects of life that satisfy the emptiness of our souls.

QUERIES FOR FURTHER REFLECTION

- How much reflection, rest and time with others are built into your life? What activities or pressures keep you from making time for reflection and community? How could you ease the burden of someone else who does not have the luxury of accepting the limits of fatigue— a single parent perhaps?

- How do you feel about aging? Is pressure to stay youthful a good motivation for health? How does it compromise your ability to be content with the realities of living long?

- What can you fast from this week, to help you take it less for granted and to remind you of your dependency on God?

- What would it mean for you to appreciate resources that are finite? How might Jesus approach life here, now? If contentment comes from living as Jesus would, what might that look like when it comes to resources, free time and work?

- How has living in a country that encourages self-determination inclined you to control your life in ways that make you demanding and discontent? How do you subtly or overtly try to control others? Your circumstances? Family gatherings?

- "The wise throughout history have always believed that contentment came not from having more things but from wanting the right things." What do you want?

- Exercise: How do you tend to push back natural limits to get more time, energy or comfort? Give one of them up for a week or a month, and look for some unexpected blessing in doing so.

SIPPING AND SAVORING

What folly not to breathe the air, walk with unfaltering step in open
country, find water in a flood; not to discover God,
not to savour him, not to perceive his bounty in all things!

JEAN-PIERRE DE CAUSSADE

Farmers work hard—especially in the summers when the sun shines long and the planting and harvesting work is most demanding. George Poynor, a colleague at Wheaton College, grew up in a small farming community. In the evenings, work ceased and rest and play commenced. George's family ate a large and leisurely dinner together at day's end and then often spent the evening visiting neighbors or receiving visitors. The adults told stories; the children sat at their feet and listened. George describes his childhood this way:

> For me these neighborly visits were magical times, and the stories adults would tell highlights in my life. On such occasions my brothers and I would implore my father, "Daddy, tell the one about . . ." desiring to hear some stories over and over and over again.

These built connections between us and things that had happened in our family a generation before that I still treasure. Oh! Those summer Sunday afternoons . . . arms aching from turning the handle on the ice cream churn, and the battles over who would get to clean ice cream off the beater . . . and those crisp winter evenings when Mother would make taffy, and we'd pull and pull, and then eat and eat.

George's family lived by the cycles of day and night, winter, spring, summer and fall. He cherishes the memories of those days, of living by the rhythms of the day and year.

That cats purr when they are content makes me smile—a reminder that contentment is physical, experienced in bodies made of muscle and bone that respond to internal rhythms and external cues including rest as well as activity. Just beneath our consciousness we inhale and exhale, constantly resupplying our body with oxygen. The heart's cycle is one of rest and activity; its chambers fill with blood, then contract, pushing oxygenated blood into our body and oxygen-depleted blood back to our lungs. Hearts rest, fill, contract, rest, beating to a rhythm that undergirds our moment-by-moment life.

Bodies tend to respond to the natural rhythms of the created world, desiring sleep when it is dark, waking to the light of day. This cadence encourages rest as well as activity. The active part we have down fairly well. Contented souls I have observed have also learned the art of sipping and savoring—experiencing life slowly with a leisurely mindfulness.

THE BUZZ OF ELECTRONIC RHYTHMS

Mesmerized by the powerful technology that eases our work, many of us live in an electronic buzz that drowns out the quiet cadence calling us to rest. We're an on-the-go plugged-in society connected by our cell phones, faxes and the Internet so we can conduct business, shop, bank, acquire information and entertain ourselves nonstop.

The quiet cadence of rest calls us to contentment, to open spaces to sip and savor life in the midst of our busyness. Sometimes hearing the cadence of rest requires us to turn down the volume of sounds competing for our attention. Like the television.

Eventually someone in George Poynor's rural neighborhood purchased a television. He says:

> My first experience of television occurred when a family who lived half a mile away got the first television set for miles around. I was about ten and would on rare occasions visit and watch *Captain Video* with the boy of my age in that family. The program consisted of a field of flickering dots, and on occasion a barely discernible image, accompanied by voices that referred to things we could hardly make out on the tiny screen. I was not impressed. My friend did say that there were times, usually late at night when all good children were in bed, when the images were very lifelike. I never got to see that phenomenon.

Eventually most of the neighbors got televisions and gave up neighborly visits in each other's home. Instead people sat around little boxes that emitted squiggly lines with tinny sounds punctuated by prerecorded laughter. The introduction of television changed the character of his community, and George grieved the transformation brought by this irresistible technology.

George is currently the director of computing services at Wheaton College. He works with technology every day, but still he says, "I have a whole passel of memories that flood back when I think about times without technology—no car, no running water, no indoor plumbing, no television, and thanks be to God, no computers!"

Television is now an assumed household appliance for most of us. Some, like George, refuse to own one. Another noise breaking loudly into quiet spaces comes from cell phones, a particularly invasive technology. Cell phones take people out of the present moment they are sharing with others and transport their attention to some virtual place instead, often resulting in their becoming mindless of those around them. Yet as with the introduction of the television fifty years ago, we are drawn toward this new technology. It allows us to talk with anyone anywhere, anytime. And it allows us to be available to others anywhere, anytime. A lifeline and a tether. Our constant accessibility means we hear the buzz of cell phones in coffee shops, restaurants, waiting rooms, movie theaters, classrooms and church sanctuaries—breaking into quiet spaces better left undisturbed.

At an airport gate one day I was journaling, finding a quiet way to use the unexpected open time presented by the delay of our flight. Already the Daily Bad News Report broadcast from suspended televisions challenged anyone's capacity to concentrate or to think good and lovely thoughts. The gentleman next to me was not interested in the news, quiet or solitude. Rather, he talked incessantly and loudly on his cell phone to someone he supervised in the sales business. He chastised, gave instructions, made demands—all in a patronizing I'm-really-your-buddy tone—and then demanded that a certain report be done when he arrived in Chicago. He hung up for a few minutes, checked on the flight, grew weary of the silence and then called his employee back. He literally did 95 percent of the talking, and this time I (and all around me) learned about his golf game, his night on the town, the women, the sales and how to climb to the top professionally. The conversation, colored with profanity, left little to the imagination.

I felt as sorry for the man on the other end of the line as I did for myself. After he hung up a second time, he tried to engage me in conversation. Since I was now failing miserably at journaling, I had resorted to writing—in a rather irritated script—cruel but honest (I rationalized) observations about this man's demeanor. I brushed him off as politely as possible given my level of agitation, whereupon he engaged in yet a third loud and lengthy call. He had no idea how irritating he was.

Five years later, cell-phone users are being made aware of the general negative effect their conversations have on those sharing space with them. A public outcry is emerging as editorials and opinion pieces debate the decision to allow cell-phone use on airplanes. Announcements in movie theaters and messages delivered by PowerPoint in church sanctuaries urge people to turn off their cell phones.

Technology that brought convenience and eased our work has expanded into every part of our lives. Sipping becomes gulping, and savoring is lost in the noise of multitasking.

GULPING AND MULTITASKING

The Protestant work ethic encouraged a strong sense of productivity in the United States. Many of us are productive and healthy members of society, participating in and volunteering at a variety of civic and religious activities, developing ourselves spiritually, emotionally and professionally, pouring ourselves into our career, earning and spending money. At the core of the Protestant work ethic is a belief that prosperity is evidence of God's favor, showing that we have been wise stewards of our time and gifts. Though most Protestants say they don't believe God's favor can be earned, we do believe we honor God by working hard.

We try to fit everything into our calendar—to live all of life simultaneously. Mark and I usually take our laptop computers whenever we leave town. Some listen to educational tapes as they sleep; many of us work at our desk while we eat our lunch. College students often feel the tension of juggling schoolwork, jobs, extracurricular activities, some sort of social life and rest. Some Christian students are also eager to serve God while in school, and they volunteer in various ministries. All of these are good activities; many of our choices are between one good and some other good.

The contented souls I've observed, however, say no to some great op-

portunities but craft space to sip and savor life. In the process they allow
the possibility of saying yes to crises that emerge—the employer who
desperately needs an extra shift covered, the volunteer coordinator
needing an extra pair of hands for the soup kitchen, the friend who
needs help with a broken car or a broken heart. If we fill our lives too
full of good opportunities, we become less available to be God's hands
and feet to minister to the unexpected.

A balance of busyness and rest is hard to achieve partly because we
think we should always be willing to care for the sick, tend the broken-
hearted and fight for justice. Wayne Muller, in *Sabbath,* calls the idea that
we should not rest because others continue to suffer a "dangerous and
corrosive myth."[1] The sabbath, he says, is a necessary reminder that
there is a time and season for everything—renewal and refreshment as
well as labor and work. Sabbath liberates us from feeling as if we must
solve all the problems of the day and see each thing through to the end
before we can rest.

The God-given human rhythm is marked by four distinct beats:
preparation, active labor, enjoying the harvest, and waiting or rest.
These are present in the sweeping pattern of seasons and in the daily
cycle of sleep and wakefulness. Poets and writers sometimes describe
our life in terms of one lifelong seasonal cycle. We prepare for life during the spring of childhood; "come of age" in summer, as we finish our
preparation and begin our life's labor; the fall comprises years of productivity and enjoying the fruits of our labor; and in the winter of old
age we rest, eat from the harvest we have sown and contemplate life.
The imagery is powerful, and the prose and poetry often beautiful. But
we misunderstand the nature of seasons when we think only in terms
of one lifelong cycle that includes a forty-five-year stretch of nonstop
productivity.

Rhythms are not about progress, and life is less about progressing toward some end point than about observing, learning and loving well on

the journey itself. Rhythms renew us, offering a structure that includes renewal, rest and reflection to prepare us for challenge, labor and productivity. When we pay attention to what is present in this moment, we acknowledge that life's rhythms bring, in turn, boring, energizing, productive, painful and joyful times. And all are sacred. Attending to rhythms gives contentment room to expand into our life.

Every year the earth's seasons repeat themselves—finished, as it were, only to begin again. We live in short cycles and long ones—some lasting a second, a day, a week, a month, a year or a decade as we move through difficult seasons and seasons of ease, times of preparation and productivity, and seasons of waiting for the fruition of our labor, and of rest. There is a rhythm underneath much in our lives that validates cycles. Muller says that when we know the season of things, we can feel their timing and so are less inclined to push a thing to completion prematurely. We become more patient, able to wait and to see what is necessary to partner with God.

SIPPING BITTER MOMENTS

For the first holiday season following my father's death, my mother planned a two-month train trip to keep her busy visiting family and friends from Thanksgiving through what would have been their fiftieth wedding anniversary. But in early November, six months after my father died, she was diagnosed with cancer. So she put her plans on hold and came to Illinois for surgery so that her daughters could provide the care for her that she had provided our father. Her two-month adventure became a two-month trek in and out of the hospital for surgery, dealing with postsurgical complications and finally radiation treatments.

On a day I went to bring her home from a four-day hospital stay that began with an emergency-room visit on Christmas Eve, I was stopped by one of the slow, long freight trains that snake through the Chicago suburbs on their way west. The sun was setting in a late December sky as I waited, content to watch the clouds carry the day's last light slowly across the prairie. Canadian geese flew in their V-formations off toward the south, and a flock of smaller birds swirled and flew gradually northeast, disappearing into the graying skies. Usually I would be waiting with varying degrees of impatience. Trains are a constant interruption for Chicagoland residents who hold some notion that they have a schedule to keep. But for this train, for almost ten minutes, I savored the day as it moved toward night, feeling comforted by the consistency of night and day, seasons, the freedom of birds in flight, God's watchfulness.

The train represented waylaid plans and schedules—a reminder of the many ways our plans are put on hold by illness, lost relationships or lost jobs that force us to slow down, look around and see what lives amidst the ruins. The train interruption renewed me that day and reminded me of God's faithful presence with us, especially with my mother in this time of grief for my father and uncertainty about her own health. Opportunities to pause are available whenever we are stalled in our plans, waiting for some train to pass.

Mom took each day as it came, rarely complaining but willing enough to grieve losses of all sorts that confronted her during those months. She practiced fortitude, getting up every day, being thankful for life, family, friends and the truth of God's presence, even when she couldn't feel the comfort of it. Some of the moments we are given are moments we would prefer not to have to live through at all. Yet if each moment is sacred, then each can be savored for what God is doing in it, even as all creation groans for redemption.

"There is a time for everything, a season for every activity under heaven," says King Solomon in Ecclesiastes 3. He talks about a time to be born and to die, to kill and to be healed, to tear down and to rebuild, to cry and to laugh, to grieve and to dance, to search and to lose. Solomon was an ambitious king who accomplished a lot politically, economically and socially during his reign. In the winter of his own life, he reflects on it all. Just after his well-known litany of life's seasons, he writes:

> What do people really get for all their hard work? I have thought about this in connection with the various kinds of work God has given people to do. God has made everything beautiful for its own time. He has planted eternity in the human heart, but even so, people cannot see the whole scope of God's work from beginning to end. So I concluded that there is nothing better for people than to be happy and to enjoy themselves as long as they can. And people should eat and drink and enjoy the fruits of their labor, for these are gifts from God. (Eccles 3:9-13)

Given the assortment of moments—both bitter and sweet—that we will confront throughout life, and since we cannot grasp the whole scope of God's work, Solomon concludes that we should be happy and enjoy the fruits of our labor as gifts from God. Was this the voice of a cynic, or wise counsel to take time, even "productive time," from each day or week to enjoy the fruits of our labor?

Thich Nhat Hanh, a Vietnamese Buddhist monk who is a mystic, scholar and activist, has spent thirty years involved in peace work. He has evacuated the wounded from combat zones, helped hungry orphans, helped rebuild villages destroyed by bombs, and always spoken out against war and for peace. He has sipped many bitter moments. The practice of meditation—of stopping, calming and looking deeply, of being present to the moment he was in—has nourished and protected his spirit, maintaining the energy he needed to continue his work.[2]

Perhaps Solomon is suggesting that whatever our circumstances in any given season, we stop, calm ourselves and look around for gifts from God. Perhaps during a frantic day we stop a moment, sit, close our eyes and focus on the goodness of breath and life itself. Perhaps after hearing bad news we stop a moment on our way home to watch the play of children and remember the wonder and miracle of life. After our children are in bed we stop, leave laundry, bills and phone calls, and sip tea, cocoa or a glass of wine while watching the glowing embers of a fire or the gentle flicker of candle flames.

Pausing to savor the goodness of life, especially during difficult seasons, is to actively return to a rhythm that nurtures us. It is not a waste of time but a gift, a discipline that is good for our soul. And if that sounds unproductive, perhaps it is because we have forgotten how to *be* without having to *do*. In our busyness we grow weary and sometimes discouraged, and fall exhausted into our bed, eager for sleep, counting the days to the weekend, or the next vacation, or retirement. To learn comfort in *being* is to relish living without succumbing to pressure to define ourselves by what we do. We avoid filling our hours and days with busyness that makes us weary and discontent.

CARVING OUT SPACES

Mark and I have learned to sip and savor our evenings. We have discovered that after a day spent interacting with people, we long for quiet time to recharge. For this reason we have carved out a schedule that rarely includes more than one evening commitment a week. We crafted it by saying no to good opportunities and insisting that our children do likewise. (I must admit, though, that this sipping and savoring thing is easier now that our children have moved out of the house!)

I know that I am better at being present to the busy and demanding moments of my job when I balance them with slowing-down periods through my day. Eight years ago I began taking a midweek break to walk to La Spiaza, a coffee shop ten minutes from campus. I drink a mocha, journal and read, and eventually return to campus refreshed, ready to re-engage with students and colleagues. My weekly walk offers me a regular look at the effects of changing seasons as I cross through Adams Park. Sometimes I'm peeking at those effects from beneath my umbrella, sometimes while navigating packed snow. Besides offering us seasonal variety, the earth models a rhythm of dormancy and rest, productivity and growth.

My journaling-coffee-walk refocuses my desire to live in the present. It's an intentional effort to slow down, to let go of what yet needs to be done, to remind myself that I cannot and should not expect to finish everything I have to do today.

Most days when I get home, my dog Chale and I go walking, as much to slow down my pace as to invigorate hers. She takes the opportunity to re-mark the neighborhood with her pee, and we both take note of neighborhood flowers, trees and bushes, birds and critters, the patterns of melting snow, the color of changing leaves. She frequently stops to sniff the air or some bush or mound of grass—her own version of sipping and savoring life.

I slow down when I become present to the world I inhabit. Others find that listening to music, reading, napping, socializing with friends, going dancing or playing an instrument releases them from work undone and pulls them to become present to their life.

Some occupations demand a constant frenetic pace. In response to a career or job that is overwhelmingly constraining and controlling, a few choose to make radical changes to regain control of their life. Linda Breen Pierce gave up her well-paying career as a lawyer and her fast-paced affluent lifestyle in search of peace and fulfillment. She decided to spend some of her newly gained time studying others who were choosing to live simply.[3] Many she interviewed said they were looking for personal fulfillment; some had grown disenchanted with the emptiness of a consumer-driven lifestyle. Most were, or along the way became, concerned for the environment and issues of global poverty and injustice. They didn't feel deprived as they chose to live with less but felt richer for having broken free of their fast-paced, technology-rich, materialistic lifestyle. They crafted lives that encouraged sipping and savoring.

LIVING LIFE IN CHAPTERS

Most of us won't feel able or inclined to radically change our life, especially if we have dependents counting on us for care and a stable income. At times I've needed to accept that a chapter I was currently living in was necessary for now, even if that was not the way I wanted to live long term. Generally, maybe always, I had some choice in the matter. I could, after all, abandon my children.

Sometimes we choose busyness because it serves some other good. Twice a season of extreme busyness came because I wanted to be physically present to care for someone who was facing death or significant illness. Since I couldn't put my regular life on hold to do so, I juggled—at cost to family and students. I had a gracious employer; many do not. For three years I commuted an hour each way to my first college teaching position, and for four years Mark chaired and directed the Psy.D. program at Wheaton, while also involved in a rigorous research program. These choices also exerted some cost from our family.

During seasons of busyness we looked for ways to build margins around our lives, to seek rest and stay open to the wonder and delight of the moment. Hale-Bopp's Comet zipped around the earth during one such chapter, and I insisted on dragging my somewhat reluctant family outside to note its historic passing. We played basketball hoop games in our backyard, threw softballs and Frisbees, went on family vacations. Mark and I said no to almost all extracurricular church, college and civic opportunities during chapters that were already too full. We took in Saturday morning and late afternoon cross-country meets, connecting with each other as we watched our daughters run. At some point Mark and I started a midweek coffee date: we'd go out for coffee, each having thought up a question to ask the other. I learned what Mark loved about his grandmother, how he experienced high school football, his most embarrassing moment, what family vacation he most treasures and how he would title the chapters of his life.

An important qualifier about living life in chapters is that we must seek to make sure no one chapter dominates the book—at least if it's a chapter that doesn't fit the way we would like to live. Sometimes it is hard to be objective enough to figure out whether the costs and sacrifices merit staying in a busy chapter. It may help to call on family or friends to give a valuable outside perspective as we consider the benefits and liabilities of staying in a particular chapter versus starting a new one. But whether we start a new chapter or stay in our current one, we can always work toward establishing rhythms of rest.

RHYTHMS OF REST

We don't have to change careers and downsize our life to begin to attend to rhythms, for they underlie our human existence. As we wake from a night of sleep, leave for and return from work, eat dinner with family, celebrate holidays and birthdays, don an overcoat or a swimsuit, we move in and out of rhythms that mark a cadence of life we can join at any time. Sleeping, eating, seasonal rituals and the sabbath are examples of established rhythms of rest from daily life.

The gift of sleep. Time and again, studies reinforce what our mothers have been telling us for years: sleep is necessary and good for us. James Maas, a psychology professor at Cornell University who studies sleep, says good sleep is the best predictor of how long people will live and their quality of life. He also says, "Most adults are moderately to severely sleep deprived, and it affects their productivity, their work, and their relationships. . . . Your alertness, energy, performance, thinking, productivity, creativity, safety and health will be affected by how much you sleep."[4] Sleep research suggests that the best benefits of sleep come between the sixth and eighth hours of sleep.[5] Depriving the brain of sleep, Maas says, makes us "clumsy, stupid and unhealthy." Sixty percent of Americans get less than seven hours of sleep a night—the minimum needed to function well.

Sleep slows us down. Our activity, conversation and conscious thinking cease as we allow ourselves to be overtaken by a state of rest that renews our body.

About 60 percent of Americans say that at least a few nights every week they have difficulty sleeping. The stresses of our job and our relationships, worries about our children or finances, hormonal changes during menopause, erratic schedules, babies and sick children all contribute to difficulty sleeping. Wisdom from the ages—likely already passed down to us from our mothers—includes suggestions for a good night's sleep. These are reemerging as recommendations from physicians and psychologists to help people overcome sleep difficulties.

Medical and mental health professionals advise us to develop a consistent bedtime routine and to go to bed at the same time every night. These patterns cue our body to get ready for sleep. The natural world darkens and quiets at night, and when we reflect that in our home we encourage our body toward rest. We can dim lights or light candles and soften external stimulation by turning off the computer and television well before bedtime. Avoiding caffeine from late afternoon on (earlier for some) and avoiding alcohol within three hours of bedtime also help us sleep and stay asleep. And finally, while not practical for most of us most days, for a good night's rest wake when your body is ready, not to the jarring sound of an alarm.

Sleep is a gift—a daily reminder that we are frail humans that need rest. In spite of consistent research, we often dismiss this simple gift that enhances our lives. We assume we are tougher than those needing eight or nine hours of sleep a night, disciplined enough to get by on five or six. And many of us can function on five or six. But with eight we are mentally sharper, more productive, kinder and better able to respond graciously to the daily challenges of living.

Mealtime rhythm and blues. Eating nourishes our body while satisfying our palate. We can bake our apples and steam our spinach, or eat them raw. Long ago people figured out how to make cheese and wine, pasta and ice cream—a tribute to our ingenuity. We are creative eaters and we need to eat—it is a rhythm of life that sustains us.

The practice of eating three meals a day is somewhat arbitrary; that our bodies desire food at regular intervals throughout the day is not. The level of sugar in our blood, gastric juices in our digestive system and a growling stomach cue us to our need for food. Medical practitioners tell us that our bodies function best when they are nourished at regular intervals. We are encouraged to eat slowly and to rest for a while after eating. Throughout history people have combined a break from activity with food and fellowship, allowing the body time to rest while renewing it with food.

Eating can become a rhythm of sustenance and thanksgiving. We are reminded of our need for food, for the earth from which it comes and for those who provide and prepare it. In the remembering we are invited to give thanks, admitting that we are finite and rely for sustenance on others, the earth and ultimately God.

Except for special occasions, such intentional eating doesn't fit the lifestyle of most of us. We have more of a "rhythm and blues" relationship with food. People often eat whatever is handy—grabbing a granola bar and coffee to go for breakfast, plunking change into a vending machine for lunch and driving through McDonald's for a Big Mac on the way home. A lot of us obsess about everything we put in our mouth—counting calories, watching fiber content, good fats/bad fats, good carbs/bad carbs. We have an uneasy relationship with food—we have to eat it but fear it will make us fat and give us high cholesterol, diabetes or a heart attack if we don't monitor our intake of it carefully.

And yet, unlike the bodies of most animals, whose diets are rather predictable (cows eat their hay and lions their prey), human bodies digest a wide variety of foods. We can savor the sweetness of peaches, the saltiness of bacon, the sour bite of lime. We stimulate our palates with cinnamon, cloves, cayenne pepper and rosemary. Corn is transformed into tortillas, wheat into bread, and wonder of wonders, cocoa beans into chocolate! We embrace the gift of food when we eat with intention, aware of what we consume and with whom we are eating it.

The international Slow Food Movement that began in 1989 is attempting this kind of transformative thinking about food. The movement encourages us to return to the days when people ate food that was grown and raised locally, prepared with creative intention and served and eaten leisurely among friends and family. The Slow Food Movement encourages people to keep pleasure in eating linked to awareness of our food and social responsibility. It stands in direct opposition to the traditional fast-food approach to dining, food preparation and factory-farming practices, as well as those of restaurant chains such as Olive Garden, TGI Friday's and Chili's. Standardized taste and mass production of food fly in the face of a movement with a philosophy summarized as "in praise of slowness" (meaning prudence and solemnity), "in praise of rest" (meaning listening to the rhythm of life and adjusting to it), "in praise of hospitality."[6] We are invited to slow down, to choose what we eat with intention, and to gather with family and friends as we nourish our bodies with food.

During our early years of marriage we planted a garden in Tennessee. Cantaloupe, lettuce, beans, corn, potatoes, squash and cucumbers all flourished with the rich mixture of Tennessee soil and sun. We canned and froze our produce, as well as peaches and apples we picked at nearby farms. Mostly we gardened out of financial necessity, but it satisfied us to grow so much of what we ate, knowing that throughout the winter we would eat wholesome food grown in our backyard and region.

After about ten years, life got too busy for tending gardens, and the luxury of our lives gave us the option not to garden for sustenance. A few years ago, however, I became aware of how little I knew about my food and how much I took it for granted. Buying whatever was on sale, I had stopped appreciating the seasons and had been forgetting the succulence of fresh locally grown produce. So I began shopping at farmers' markets, growing my own vegetables again, and educating myself about eggs from free-range chickens and free-range pork and beef.[7] I wanted to support local farmers, be more connected to and educated about what I ate, and pay attention to the seasonal cycles required to grow it.

As I turn under the soil of my planting beds in fall, mixing in compost from garden and kitchen scraps, I am aware that farmers are tilling and nourishing their fields. The ground rests through the winter, is planted in the spring, and is weeded and watered throughout the summer and fall as they, and I, reap a harvest to sell or share with friends and neighbors. Planting my little raised beds has given me a renewed appreciation for the connection between food and rain, sun, seasons and the labor of farmers.

Even though we are an on-the-go culture, we can still weave fellowship into our rhythm of eating. When I jogged through neighborhoods in the early morning hours, I occasionally passed a house from which an aroma of bacon and eggs wafted out to me. I found it warming—a blessing of sorts—that people were taking time to fix and eat a hot meal together at the break of day.

The year we moved to Wheaton, where the high schools, middle schools and elementary schools all had different start times, was the year our family stopped eating breakfast together. To try to compensate, Mark continued his habit of taking a daughter out to breakfast one day a week, and I tried picking another up from school one day a week for lunch. But mostly we ate breakfast on our own and used lunch to connect with coworkers and friends. At dinner we reconnected as a family after a day spent going in different directions. Sometimes we took turns sharing a high point and a low point of our day. As the girls moved through middle school and high school, we told mostly bad jokes or talked about ideas they were discussing in school, or world events, or family matters.

Sports, jobs and church activities competed with this dinner ritual throughout their high school years, and we didn't work as hard as we could have to protect it. But when we managed it, eating together allowed us to connect with each other, to pause from our individual lives and come together, reminding ourselves that we belonged to something larger than ourselves that needed protecting.

Sometimes I still fall into the snare of working through lunch, eating at my desk as I grade papers or answer e-mails, trying to cram as much efficiency into my day as possible. I need to remind myself that having a "productive" day is not as satisfying as a day in which I took time to stroll across campus instead of rush and to be fully present during conversations with colleagues and students, not distracted by tasks that needed attention. There is always more to do—reading, preparing, phone calls and e-mails to answer, errands to run, appointments to make. Letting go of some grandiose idea that we can finish it all lets us break from our labor simply to eat.

Our culture isn't set up for sipping and savoring meals. But we can make eating a more meaningful part of our day by protecting it as an opportunity to slow down, to be more intentional about what we eat and where it comes from, and to seek ways to build fellowship into our eating.

Seasonal rituals. Rituals call our attention to the present and encourage us to be mindful of the underlying activity of a particular season. A favorite fall activity of mine is to go out to one of the forest preserves on a windy day and stand among the trees as they rain down leaves in their final dance with wind. The tree is about to enter a time of dormancy, when growth ceases. The leaves have done their work, carrying the sun's energy to the tree, and are released back to the earth, where they will return to soil, nourishing the tree in years to come. To stand among falling leaves is to remember my own need to let go, to trust the work I have done this day, this week, this semester or this year is sufficient and will continue to bring some good in days to come.

In the Midwest, seasons are definite, with clearly distinct markers of a cycle moving through time. Something almost ritualistic happens after the first big snowfall. In the early darkness of a late afternoon or evening, neighbors returning from work accept the invitation of winter—already accepted by the neighborhood children—to come walk or play in the snow. Later we call greetings to each other as we shovel driveways and sidewalks. Likewise, on the first warm days of spring, people move outside to walk or bike or to sit on their porch, again greeting each other after the cold of winter that kept us mostly snuggled inside our homes.

Sometimes rituals of remembrance are simply observations of change accompanied by delight, honoring the world we inhabit by paying attention to the cadence of its rhythms. We can choose to see snow as a traffic problem, falling leaves as a nuisance, spring as a wet and muddy disappointment, and the heat of summer as something to escape and complain about. Or we can take delight in the changing seasons. In the Midwest and East, that means spring peepers come out from hibernation, exploding in sound. They announce that winter is giving way to spring as they call to each other from across marshes and ponds. Robins build nests, often in trees or eaves, and then hatch and feed their young right outside our windows. We can sit outside after dark and watch the first fireflies of June, walk in the warmth of sultry summer nights and then, all too soon, in the crisp air of a fall morning. Rain turns to snow. Everything sleeps. And then it all reawakens; trees, perennials, bulbs and spring peepers. To observe is to be present to the moment, content and delighted in the gift of changing seasons.

Different regions and communities have their own markers that announce change and offer invitations to celebrate the coming and passing of seasons. The winter and summer solstices (the "shortest" and "longest" days of the year) have been celebrated for thousands of years by cultures around the world—in ancient Egypt and medieval Europe, and by the Mayan Indians of what is now Mexico. The winter solstice, occurring between December 20 and 22, began the solar year. People celebrated by exchanging gifts and greetings, decorating their home with lights, giving to the needy and putting out seeds for birds. The summer solstice (June 20-22) is still celebrated in communities around the world, often with the lighting of bonfires, outdoor dancing, singing and games.

Days set aside for thanksgiving feasts have long served for community celebrations of the abundance of the harvest season. New Year celebrations have generally replaced ancient winter solstice celebrations, but both herald the ending of one year and the beginning of the next. On February 2, Punxsutawney Phil, the official U.S. groundhog, gives the word on how much winter we have left.[8]

As we engage in community-held celebrations, we pause from our work and step into an awareness of the seasons that give structure to our daily routines and have done so throughout human history. We are creatures of a world that cycles through seasons, and we are created to share a rhythm that moves us from preparation to productivity to rest.

Saving the sabbath. "Sabbath is a day we walk in the forest, walk among the fruits of our harvest and the ruins of our desperations, and see what lives," says Wayne Muller.[9] In the Genesis creation story, God rests on the seventh day. God's rest is a sign of completion and abundance.[10] We are invited into a sabbath rest to acknowledge our dependence on the God who sustains us. All our productivity is small potatoes compared to the good gifts of God. Perhaps knowing that the Israelites (and other human beings) would not be inclined to follow the rhythm of the seasons, God etched a day of rest into the Ten Commandments that would guide our lives, encouraging us to celebrate, to rest, to walk among the fruits of our labor and the ruins of our desperations, and to see what lives.

For Israel, on the sabbath work was to cease for everyone, including servants and foreigners (Ex 20:8-11). Women did not cook; provisions for food were made ahead of time. Even the land was to be given a year of total rest, a sabbath every seventh year when crops were not planted nor vineyards pruned (Lev 25:1-7). While Jesus accused Jewish leaders of missing the point when they condemned him for healing a man on the sabbath (Lk 6), our error is often at the opposite extreme—to disregard the sabbath entirely, assuming it is a leftover Jewish law that Jesus abolished.

Sabbath rest invites us to pause, to reflect on where we have been and where we are going. The Israelites did so in the context of worship, being mindful of the God who created and sustained them and for whose glory and honor they lived.

For the first half of the twentieth century, a day of rest and worship continued to be observed in U.S. communities as businesses and many stores and restaurants closed on Sunday, allowing employees to go to church and to be home with their family. A drive to make the most of economic opportunities eventually dictated new public norms and traditions that encouraged commerce on Sunday. People generally had more time and energy to spend money on the weekends, and not to provide opportunities for them to do so wasted a moneymaking opportunity. This was especially true as women, the primary shoppers, were increasingly tied up with day jobs during the week. Now Sunday is a day much like any other—people shop, run errands, dine out, and attend sporting and entertainment events, filling a day of rest and community worship for souls with an assortment of activities for consumers.

People who uphold the sabbath cease from doing that which they perceive as work. Some people uphold the spirit of the sabbath by not spending money on their day of rest, wanting to refrain from participating in activities that require others to work on the sabbath. Some of my colleagues observe the sabbath by not grading papers, preparing lectures, answering e-mails or turning on their computer on Sunday. They model sabbath keeping for students and encourage them to schedule their study throughout the week so they can observe a day of rest. Some cease from exercising on the sabbath; others find ways to exert themselves physically because activity is what brings a break from their sedentary workday life.

When I observe the sabbath, the weekend nears with a ready anticipation. I know my grading/teaching/advising/administrating/prepping work will end and that rest waits. The sabbath will likely include some mulling over the week, thinking back through words read or spoken, questions asked or answered that I hadn't had time to reflect on more fully. A sabbath rest will often include physical activity that allows me to sip and savor the gifts of whatever season we're in. I'll work in the yard, pick apples and make applesauce or a cobbler, make soup or bake bread, take a long walk, sit and watch a fire while drinking tea. I try to protect as much of the weekend from my occupational work as I can, preferring to use it for household tasks that I enjoy when I can do them in a leisurely way.

Observing the sabbath looks different given the various times of life, occupations and schedules we have. Family caregivers can't easily take a complete day of rest, for every day they are preparing meals, cleaning up and caring for others, helping with doctor's visits, school projects and extracurricular activities. Similarly, people with jobs that require them to work irregular schedules have a difficult time taking a consistent sabbath rest.

In *Sabbath Keeping*, Lynne Baab encourages us to find creative ways to craft a regular twenty-four-hour day of rest and to change it to adapt to the seasons of life. She encourages us to become free from doing anything that would appear on a to-do list or things that would be judged by their progress or production. It is a day free from multitasking, so that one cooks (if one enjoys it) with slow attention to the process, or one watches a child's sporting event without taking a laptop, cell phone or papers. The sabbath gives us permission to set aside whatever we feel is essential to accomplish and to remember that the God who sustains us is abundant and sufficient. Sabbath rest is one of God's good gifts, a discipline intended to bless us.

Some of the people lawyer-turned-author Linda Breen Pierce studied said their increasing frustration with the lack of rest and control they had over their daily schedule led to their radical changes. They curtailed children's extracurricular activities and found jobs with hours more compatible to the family's schedule, even if it meant downsizing and living more simply with less. While radically altering our life isn't feasible or desirable for all of us, we can apply sabbath principles wherever we are.

The basic sabbath principle is a call to rest. People who work weekends can observe a day of rest during the week. As Jewish women planned ahead, preparing meals for the sabbath the day before, parents can plan ahead and minimize what they do for their children so they all can have a day of rest. Children at various ages can be brought into preparations for sabbath and taught early in life to honor a day of rest. Homework and preparation for school on Monday can be completed on Saturday. A time of rest can be scheduled into an afternoon, with everyone required to either nap or be engaged in a quiet activity, alone or together.

Taking a sabbath rest renews us so that we can be more attentive, patient, caring and productive during the week. We are created to live in cycles, with seasons of preparation and of productivity, times of enjoying the fruits of our labor and times of rest. To attempt to sustain a long season of productivity is costly and ultimately counterproductive. A sabbath offers a weekly opportunity to rest from our labors, though it is primarily a reminder that we are to stop and give thanks to God, who sustains us and on whom we depend.

A second sabbath principle is a call for corporate worship and fellowship. Generally, churchgoing Christians observe the sabbath by coming together for worship. In doing so we remind ourselves of the hope that sustains us because God loves us, and we respond with praise and thanksgiving. The rest of the day is generally up for grabs. Zach, a graduate student who rented our basement apartment during grad school, regularly observed Sunday as a day of rest. He looked forward to enjoying the company of fellow students and friends on Sunday afternoon and evening. But often his friends used the afternoon and evening for studying, and he had to look elsewhere for fellowship. How different sabbath feels for those who live in communities where everyone responds together, entering a day of rest that frees them to come together to play games, visit and share recreation. The sabbath was not given to individual Israelites, remember, but to Israel as a community.

A WORD ABOUT WORSHIP

Sipping and savoring life is an act of worship. Contentment comes as we relish the mercies God pours out in daily life. The food we eat, the sleep that renews us, work, play, the celebrations we participate in, the creative capacities we exercise—all these good gifts call us to praise and worship God. In the Psalms, King David praises God for creating and sustaining the world, even as he cries out to God for mercy or salvation. Paul often ends his letters with reminders to be joyful, to keep praying and to always give thanks (see Phil 4:4; 1 Thess 5:16-18). We are urged to be mindful and watchful of God's life-sustaining mercies and gifts.

To get up early to watch a sunrise, to stop activity long enough in the evening to watch the sunset and to give thanks for God's faithfulness in sustaining our movement through space is an act of worship. Some learn the names of and then identify trees, birds or stars, and are thankful to a creative God as they do. Some are drawn to worship as they climb mountains or forge streams, or dig among their vegetables or flowers. Making or listening to music, writing or reading poetry or fiction, painting or pottery making can all be acts of worship if we perform them with a sense of awe at the creative God whom we emulate. Caring for and loving others, being God's hands and feet of mercy to both strangers and kin, is perhaps our highest act of worship.

Worship becomes a way of life, not just something we do for an hour on Sunday mornings. As we walk through our days, we choose to be mindful of the wonders around us, even amidst disappointment. We extend kindness, listen to each other, bear each other's burdens, do our work thoroughly and play wholeheartedly. Worship beckons us to be actively engaged with the world as God's image bearers called to love mercy, do justice and walk humbly with God (Mic 6:8). Our heart is quickened by God's good creation and a rhythm of thanksgiving that brings contentment to our soul.

We often do these acts of worship alone, but we are also called to come together in worship and to encourage each other toward a life of hope, love and thanksgiving. We sing songs of praise, we repent, ask for help, pray and listen to wise instruction. There is a corporate rhythm to worship as well as an individual one, and we are strengthened as we come together regularly. The writer of Hebrews says:

> Without wavering, let us hold tightly to the hope we say we have, for God can be trusted to keep his promise. Think of ways to encourage one another to outbursts of love and good deeds. And let us not neglect our meeting together, as some people do, but encourage and warn each other, especially now that the day of his coming back again is drawing near. (Heb 10:23-25)

Sipping and savoring God's creation—which includes each other, plants and animals, the seasons, night and day, oceans and mountains—keeps us mindful of the mercies of God. We are part of a creation moving to a grand cadence that invites us to be present to each moment, enjoying our work, the fruits of our labor and rest. Activity is an important part of life, and when it moves into and out from quietness, a rhythm emerges that draws us toward greater contentment.

QUERIES FOR FURTHER REFLECTION

- What is your relationship to the television? your cell phone? your computer? How much do these influence your day-to-day routines, your rhythms, your focus?

- "Life is less about progressing toward some end point than about observing, learning and loving well on the journey itself." Do you believe this? How does your life reflect it?

- Does your life have enough openness and flexibility so that you can be "available to be God's hands and feet to minister to the unexpected"?

- What spaces have you carved out of your regular routines for rest, for savoring life? For instance, how much sleep do you *actually* get most nights? Is it enough? What's your attitude toward food and eating?

- How have you observed (or not observed) the sabbath, and what is your rationale? Do you need to rethink sabbath keeping?

- Exercise: Are you satisfied with your current chapter? If you could change something significant (job, lifestyle choices, various activities) so you had more time for savoring life and relationships, what might that look like? What would it cost you and your family, and what would you and your family gain in return?

7

WALKING GENTLY

Recall that whatever lofty things you might accomplish today, you will do
them only because you first ate something that grew out of dirt.

BARBARA KINGSOLVER

One day I bring Dixie cups into my Intro to Sociology class and ask for three volunteers. I always have several brave hearts who raise their hands. I tell them to give me saliva samples, and with the class watching, they do their best, some managing quite a bit better than others. Meanwhile the rest of us talk about the merits of saliva—the good that it does for our digestive tract and its role in keeping our mouths moist. After agreeing that this is a valuable fluid, I ask if anyone wants to drink from one of these cups to boost their own saliva supply. Of course no one does—nor do the original donors care to swallow back their own.

We talk about why valuable saliva quickly becomes so very undesirable. Soon the students decide that while saliva may be a good fluid, it becomes spit (a decidedly *bad* fluid) once it leaves the body. People spit at others to insult them; we spit out unpleasantness. Spit, we agree, is not nearly so redemptive as saliva. Our conversation turns to the power of names and naming—how the meanings and values and nature of our relationship to a thing are reflected in what we call it.

The same discussion could be had about soil (good) and dirt (bad), though it wouldn't be nearly so provocative for my students. We plant an assortment of vegetables and flowers in soil; dirt merely creates dust in our house and spots on our carpets. Defining dirt as a nuisance gives us permission to do whatever we want with land. If we choose to farm it, we call the ground "soil" and treat it with care; if we want to build a parking lot, we call the ground "dirt" and pave over it. Five acres of ground can be used to grow corn or turned into a strip mall with parking.

Our perception of creation is much the same. We can define the earth as a resource to subdue, use and control since we believe we were given dominion over it. Or we can define the earth as a sacred space, God's creation that we are to care for, preserve and conserve. A characteristic I observe in contented souls is a tendency to define creation as sacred, bringing an obligation and expectation that they treat it with respect and care.

Contentment and care for creation are interwoven strands emerging from who we are: image bearers of God and dust of the earth. As creatures of the earth, we have been given the capacity to respond to and comprehend the wonders of creation. As image bearers of God, we've been given the role of caretaker, an obligation born out of our nature. Contentment is a byproduct of living rightly, properly understanding our obligatory relationship to creation.

The wonders of the earth call out, inviting those who are mindful— who hear, see, taste and smell—to praise and honor God, whose creation brings us pleasure and sustenance. Gratitude and obligation take tangible form as we walk gently amid God's creation. A life of gratitude becomes a life characterized by contentment, and contentment calls forth our gratitude.

I'm not suggesting we tear down all our parking lots and shopping malls and plant trees (though I must admit the idea has some appeal to me). God knew we would put our minds to work to order and organize

the world. We have reason, intelligence and the capacity as social creatures to coordinate efforts and to pass knowledge from one generation to
the next. We discovered how to make steel and concrete, harness electricity, use electromagnetic energy for wireless communication systems
and use microscopic technologies to develop biogenetic engineering.
Building, organizing, discovering is good, but as we discover and invent
we are to be stewards, caretakers of God's creation.

There were alternative paths we could have taken with our discover-
ies and inventions. I wonder how the world might have looked if those
of us with power to shape the world had defined our relationship to the
earth differently.

Contented souls walk gently, staying mindful of and respecting God's
creation: humans, the living things with whom we share the earth and
the earth from which we draw sustenance. But walking gently is a challenge. To pave or not to pave? To develop or preserve? At one end of this
conversation, there are the Amish, who embrace many limits and walk
gently on the earth out of respect for God, for the sake of their community and to uphold their life values.

Those at the other end push humanity forward using any technologies possible to overcome the limits of our physical existence. At the extreme is a posthuman perspective that assumes humanity is forever becoming better at improving on our physical existence. Our obligation is
to use science and technology to move us into a better future, one less
dependent on our bodies and the limits of nature. According to University of California professor N. Katherine Hayles, a posthuman perspective considers our human dependence on biological matter as an accident of history rather than essential to what it means to be human. Our
ability to invent and use information is the key factor in our progress.
The body has been helpful insofar as we have used it to manipulate our
environment, to build machines capable of achieving far more than a human could. Hayles says we will eventually be seamlessly connected to in-

telligent machines. In the posthuman state, there aren't significant differences or absolute points where our body ends and technology begins as we go about the business of living.[1]

Alarm bells start going off for me (and a whole lot of other people). What most of us fear about this idea or goal is losing the significance of being human. Hayles seeks to calm our fears by suggesting that this is an overreaction that comes from assuming there are clear boundaries between our bodies and the technology we use to make our bodies more effective. We are already headed toward posthumanity, according to Hayles, with our dependence on computer technology, cell phones and the Internet— extensions of our humanity that far increase our capabilities. She suggests that embedding microchips in our bodies for a variety of purposes is not far off.

I'm still not buying it. Besides that it gives me the heebie-jeebies, this perspective is far from a Christian conception of human nature and human dignity in which our bodies, and all created matter, are held to be sacred. From the posthuman perspective, matter doesn't matter; rather, information about matter matters. But social and physical scientists, philosophers and writers are skeptical, concerned about the implications of a posthuman vision.

Gattaca, a 1997 science fiction movie, explores a world where genetically enhanced humans inherit privilege and opportunity while the naturally born, because of their human limitations, are employable only as service workers. Frailty is weeded out and humanity perfected. In this world, to be content requires perfection, and dignity is achieved through improving the human specimen, using available technology to eradicate weakness. If we are headed toward a posthuman future, current storytellers send us with a warning that an important piece of humanity may get lost when eradicating all human flaws becomes the human norm.

Some, like Hayles, would argue that such apocalyptic predictions are exaggerations. For instance, progress made possible through genetic engineering dignifies our humanity by using human intelligence to allow us to continue stretching toward bettering ourselves and our circumstances.

Most of us live in between these two perspectives, attracted to neither end of the spectrum. We love nature, but we also love our cell phone and our indoor plumbing. How do we determine if we are walking gently enough? Contentment blends gratitude and pleasure at the good gifts of creation (including some technology developed along the way) with responsible decision making that considers the impact and implications of our choices. Contentment is not passive. Recognizing God's presence and constant movement toward redemption, we respond by living courageously, responsibly and well.

My particular challenge is to keep from growing overly disgruntled and discontented in a country I perceive to be reeling out of control in its love of technology and consumption of resources. Members of my family put up graciously with my efforts to woo them back from the temptations of technology. We negotiate where we set the thermostat (and my use of morning and evening summer breezes as I open and shut windows and shades throughout the day), and Mark puts up with my sometimes over-the-top measures to consume less, reuse and recycle— like attempts to get multiple uses from any "disposable" container that makes its way into our home. Sometimes, though, my enthusiasm can be alienating. When I insist that everyone do things my way, I become critical and ungracious. When I become cynical about living in a country that takes environmental issues lightly compared to most of the rest of the world, contentment and gratitude ebb away. Contentment is remembering that God is present, ultimately in control and working to bring balance, to transform and restore that which is broken. Contentment requires that I express gratitude for the small miracles that do occur— many communities now have recycling programs, and increasingly people are becoming mindful of a need to consume less—even as I hope for and appropriately encourage greater mindfulness in myself and my fellow citizens.

So how do I know if I'm walking gently—or gently enough? One potential starting place is to ask collectively what matters to us. Can we, as communities of faith, explore our relationship to God's creation, and what about that matters regarding how we live?

A THEOLOGY OF THE BODY

Walking gently begins with having a good theology of the body. We are souls, and souls are sacred.

Our bodies can taste, see, hear, touch, feel pain and pleasure, move and manipulate things. We can bask in the sultry heat of a summer evening and splash in puddles left by a summer rain. During a week in the Ozarks, Mark and I savored the smell of sautéing onions and peppers that later accompanied the steak grilling outside. We felt the coolness of a breeze caress our hot skin as we hiked around Leatherwood Lake, and late one night were entertained by the resounding thunder and pounding rain of a late spring storm. Pleasure comes to us through our physical bodies.

We also experienced the itch of chigger bites, the pain of burnt pale skin exposed to too much sun and the indigestion caused by eating too much of a good thing. A broken toe or a charley horse slows us down, and we find it hard to stay pleasant, engaged and on task when pain in our head pulses to the beat of our heart. We have physical bodies that feel pleasure and pain.

Our bodies can build snow forts that last a few days or city walls that last a millennium. We've taken journeys across deserts on camels, across oceans on boats, through forests on snowshoes and to the moon on Apollo 11. Those who explore the heavens open up the mysteries of an ever-expanding universe, and those studying subatomic particles remind us that we (and all matter) are largely made up of empty spaces and energy sustained by a force that defies simple explanation. On some primordial level, contentment involves tangible gratitude, embracing a simplicity that allows us to appreciate matter—our bodies in their raw, flawed and beautiful state, and the physical world, however altered by the course of human history.

Christians believe the source of human dignity comes from God, who gave dignity to our physical bodies in at least three ways. First, we are *imago Dei*— made in God's image and mirroring God in our creative, rational and relational natures. Second, when "the Word became human and lived here on earth among us" (Jn 1:14), God dignified the frailty and sacred loveliness of the human body by becoming like us in physical form. Third, we hold the hope of a bodily resurrection, in which one day we will be restored to a perfect embodied state.

The miraculous gift of the incarnation dignifies human existence and struggle. Jesus did not come to perfect humanity by getting rid of all misery and struggle; rather, he experienced hunger, thirst and weariness and ultimately died an agonizing death. Jesus, who can identify with our suffering, taught us the beauty of extending mercy, living with grace, integrity and fortitude in limited and frail human bodies.

Christian doctrine rejects Gnosticism, the belief that the physical body is a burden and a barrier to maturity and needs to be overcome by the intellect. Gnosticism led people to disregard and distrust both pleasure and pain and to focus only on immaterial physical states that transcended physical experiences. This body-denying idea rejects rather than embraces the physical nature of our humanity.

Christians also reject radical dualism—the idea that humans have two separate natures, physical and spiritual. We cannot separate our physical experience from our spiritual one. I do not merely *have* a soul; I *am* a soul. My body's experience of pain or pleasure is my soul's experience of the same. According to our Christian faith, our human dignity comes from being physical, embodied creatures that bear the image of God. God declared our body good, and the lived experience of our body and spirit are intertwined. We are souls, and souls are sacred.

ECONOMIC JUSTICE

But it is not only *our* body that has dignity. It is *every* body. As Christians we are called to care about injustices done on other bodies by becoming informed about parts of life we would rather not see. For instance, many of our diamonds come from Africa, and many of these are "conflict diamonds" from mines in Sierra Leone. The mines are controlled by rebel groups, who use brutal force to make villagers extract the gems. They then sell these diamonds to major American and European jeweler companies and use the money to support their uprisings against internationally recognized governments in various parts of Africa.[2] When we buy such diamonds, whether or not we know it, we are participating in injustice.

Another example is the disruption of traditional ways of life in less developed parts of the world. Corrupt and legitimate governments both take land that has been farmed by local people for centuries and turn it over to multinational corporations that are looking to reduce labor and production costs for textile, electronic and food-processing enterprises. With no one to hold them accountable, corporations set up sweatshops that are illegal in the developed world, thereby enhancing their profits. The work can be hazardous, the hours long and the pay inadequate to cover basic human needs. For subsistence farmers who have lost their farms, sweatshop labor is one of only a few paths that remain open to make a living. Hearing there is work in the city, poor people from the countrysides migrate to urban centers, adding to already crowded and unsanitary conditions there and an unemployment rate that drives down wages for sweatshop labor.

The CEOs of these multinational corporations are not necessarily evil; they believe they are acting in the best interest of their shareholders, investors like you and me. The CEO's job is to maximize our profit, and they do their job well.[3] But in the process they contribute to the world's evil and pain. Today grassroots organizations are mobilizing and calling on CEOs to consider the ethical implications of doing their job well.

Capitalism is an economic system that encourages everyone to own something defined as "valuable," such as money, precious metals or stones, property and stock. The idea of owning land, trees, animals and other people emerged long before capitalism. As small hunting and gathering clans evolved into herding and farming communities, they became increasingly inclined to enlarge their territories by conquering other people groups and taking or making claim on what belonged to others. Property ownership became a defining characteristic as civilizations became more complex—the driving force behind colonialism and expansion. Native Americans, however, believed they belonged to the earth rather than the other way around; they didn't see the land as something human beings could own. And so land rights, as we defined them, were easily taken away from them. Even then, Native Americans didn't always understand that land now "belonging" to white folks was no longer open for them to fish and hunt on.

We are not used to thinking of ourselves as belonging to the earth or being obligated to others with whom we share it. Rather, the earth belongs to us—particularly the piece of land we may happen to officially "own," or some precious metal, diamond or stock that we have managed to secure. We don't see ourselves as particularly accountable to the rest of the world for our purchases. Thinking this way makes it easy to disregard issues of economic justice for others.

A theology of the body encourages us to see ourselves as part of creation, obligated to care for the earth even as we draw sustenance from it. Walking gently means that we strive for justice for all inhabitants of the earth and make choices that bring good rather than ill. If every body deserves human dignity, then we will live, as much as is possible, in ways that do not deny dignity to others or bring them harm.

Much of the harm we cause is related to the stuff we buy and consume. *The Better World Handbook* and the Internet resource <www
.responsibleshopper.org> are examples of guides for individuals seeking
to make small or large changes to live in ways consistent with their values regarding economic justice, strengthening communities and ecological well-being.[4]

ECOLOGICAL HEALTH

Walking gently is usually linked to our relationship with the earth.
When my family lived in Tucson, Arizona, my father often took us on
miniadventures that helped us come to love the world in an up-close and
personal way. On one family hike we found a cave in Cochise Canyon.
We explored the wonders of this pristine cavern, which seemed, in my
little-girl world, to go on forever. At one point we had to crawl one at a
time down through a narrow opening that then opened into a huge cavern where our words echoed back at us in the dark. I thought of Jill in
The Silver Chair, one of C. S. Lewis's Narnia books, who was forced to
crawl through the tunnels of the Underworld, and my heart pounded
like hers in the utter darkness. Dad turned on the flashlight, showing the
depth and breadth of the cavern and the small cold pool of water at the
bottom that we could climb down to and touch.

Exploring the world connects me to the lives of others who have gone
before me—other hikers, explorers, native people who lived in these
caves or those mountains, or beside riverbeds, long before we turned
these lands into state or national parks. I am reminded of the long stream
of humanity from which I come and how people lived with limits, yet
how much more they understood about the basic skills needed to live
well. I sense an obligation to learn about this world and ultimately to
leave it a better place, to leave a testimony of God's presence and power
to those who come after me.

When I appreciate the gift of creation and recognize the abundant and good blessings in it, I want to walk gently on it, to leave a small footprint, to use resources carefully. This doesn't feel like a sacrifice but a desire that comes from love of God's creation. People who live gently leave a legacy that shows they have walked respectfully of the earth, mindful of those who came before them and those who will come after them.

It is difficult for us in the United States to walk gently on the earth, where the size of the average "ecological footprint" (how much productive land and water we need to support what we use and what we discard) is twenty-four acres per person. Feeling some pride for being environmentally conscientious, I decided to take a quiz one day to see how well I was doing.[5] It asked questions like how big my house was and how many people live in it, how often I ate meat, whether I drove, carpooled, used public transportation or walked to work, and how often I fly across the country or the world. To my dismay, I discovered that twenty-one acres are required to sustain my lifestyle. Since there are only 4.5 biologically productive acres per person in the world, we would need 4.7 planets to sustain us all if everyone lived the way I do. The test isn't a perfect indicator of how environmentally conscientious we are being, but it raised my awareness about resource use I hadn't thought about. Since becoming aware of the size of my footprint, I am seeking ways to shrink it—to do my small part in using less.

The Voluntary Simplicity movement reemerged in the early 1990s as people evaluated their stressful, fast-paced lives and increasing debt as they tried to afford the U.S. lifestyle. Like those in Linda Breen's study, people in the Voluntary Simplicity movement say that in the process of slowing down they discover a satisfaction that comes with increased time for family, friends and simple activities. Some learn to make wine; others tend orchards, selling apples, applesauce and cider. Some rediscover the art of baking, others till and plant, some become shepherds; some write or teach, or keep doing what they've always done, but on a smaller scale. They buy and use less and in the process live more gently on the earth, while gaining a sacred appreciation for the earth's good gifts that sustain them.

Ray Anderson, CEO of Interface, the world's largest commercial carpet manufacturer, became convicted of his company's damaging and exploitative use of the earth to make carpets. He rejected the misguided belief held by many in manufacturing that the earth is unlimited, both as a source for raw material and as a "limitless sink into which we can send our poisons and waste."[6] He led his company to make substantial changes in reducing the cost to the earth for every carpet made and entering into a ten-year effort to become sustainable. His company defines sustainable as being more than just environmentally friendly; rather, sustainability is "a dynamic process which enables all people to realize their potential and to improve their quality of life in ways that simultaneously protect and enhance the Earth's life support systems."[7]

Anderson's efforts affirm the dignity of all life. Perhaps if we learn the names and habits of the birds and critters that fly or scurry around our neighborhood, take note of and learn the names of plants and trees, observing how they cycle through the year—perhaps then we will fall in love with this amazing place and be content to consume less so that the offspring of all life might live well.

GOOD WORK

I spent a day with Nubian women weavers, joining them during my advisory visit to Emily, a Wheaton College student who was interning with Uganda Crafts in Kampala, Uganda, for six months. That day we joined employers of Uganda Crafts to go supervise the dyeing of reed for baskets Uganda Crafts bought from the women and sold to Ten Thousand Villages, a nonprofit organization that provides a market to the artisans and a fair and livable wage.

The women met and formally greeted us, and then invited us to sit in chairs they moved out from inside where we were given milk, tea, eggs (from their chickens) and fried potatoes (from their gardens) before we began the work of the day. We dyed reed in a vat of steaming water boiling over an open flame. Sweat dripped off our noses and ran down our backs as we tried to steer clear of the eye-burning smoke that chased us around the caldron. We stirred, flipped, lifted and eventually tossed the reed onto the grass to dry. I say "we" because they were as eager to have us participate as we were to do so.

Afterward, under the shade of trees, they demonstrated and tried to teach us some of their mat weaving and other basket-weaving techniques. They sat together on mats they had woven; women working side by side at their livelihood, threading reed through large-eyed needles and then pushing it through tiny holes in the reed and wrapping it tightly around a cluster of dried grass that formed the beginnings of what became the strong, colorful and beautifully patterned baskets for which they are known. Emily and I tried our hand at it, and we all laughed at our lumpy attempts at basket making. A few women spoke a bit of English, and Emily spoke a bit of a common language they shared, but mostly we communicated with our eyes, bodies and smiles.

Children returned from school, formally greeted elders and guests and then began the afternoon task of drawing water from the well. Before sending us on our way the women served us a wonderful meal made again from the produce gathered or cultivated from near their homes.

The work of the Nubian women is good. It provides income for their families, crafts something useful and beautiful, and fosters community by developing relationships that extend beyond work into each other's lives.

Work in the West is rather more distanced from crafting tools and performing tasks directly related to our sustenance. Increasingly we have become disconnected from the earthiness of our souls, distant from the soil, animals and raw materials that facilitate our abundant lives. One result is that I can't feed myself. That is, I don't have the land, the tools or the know-how to get from cow to steak or from wheat to bread. I buy packaged meat from the grocer, glad to be distanced from cattle raising, especially the butchering, gutting, skinning and deboning process that is the prelude to the steak, ham or chicken on our plates.

Modern life has given us useful, inventive solutions to our complex challenges, bettering life but distancing us from the ability to live simply and knowledgeably off the land. From snow blowers to clothes dryers, we have developed tools that substitute human energy with energy from electricity or gas, promising that we will sweat less, produce more and have more time for leisure. Whether or not they have freed up more time for leisure is debatable. But these devices do consume more of our time and take-home pay as we shop for, buy, assemble, use and maintain them.

Once we became consumers we generally believed the television commercials, magazine ads and billboards that told us happiness and contentment came from consuming something. We trusted inventions to better our lives. Wendell Berry has his own standards for determining whether or not he'll adopt some new technology. He believes the new tool or technology should be cheaper than the one it replaces, use less energy than the one it replaces, be repairable by a person of ordinary intelligence, be bought locally from a privately owned establishment, and not replace or disrupt anything good that already exists, including family and community relationships. His list provided a good starting place for me as I began thinking about how to blend the use of tools, natural resources and my body to do the work of living.

He also helps me critique my ideas about what constitutes "meaningful work." Walking gently grounds us through good work, connecting us to the earth on which we live as we go about our livelihood. In hunting and gathering societies, various activities we'd call "work" flowed together with family time, recreation and religion, all meaningful activities done side by side. Notions like "the forty-hour work week," "career calling" and "meaningful work" didn't exist. Eventually electricity and machines replaced much of the need for human labor, so fewer people needed to work together growing and producing food, weaving cloth, crafting baskets, tanning hides and overseeing the basic tasks of sustaining lives. We found other work deemed meaningful, because meaningful work has always contributed to our sense of well-being and contentment.

Philosophers, social scientists and religious leaders all uphold good work and good relationships as necessary components for a satisfying life. Good work, we decided collectively, produces something worthwhile—a service rendered to others or a useful or beautiful product. Meaningful work leaves the world a better place, on balance doing more good than harm.

We have peculiar notions of what makes work worthwhile in the modern world, at least if the prestige we offer as a reward is any indication. An occupational prestige scale from 2000 shows that people in the United States value physicians the most (with the highest score, 86) and janitors the least (score of 22). Farm laborers, those who produce the food the rest of us need to live, received a score of 23. Farmers fared somewhat better with a score of 40. Farmers are still beneath secretaries (46) but slightly above hairdressers (36) and truck drivers (30). Childcare workers at 36 are on par with hairdressers.[8] Useful and good work does not necessarily equal work that is admired (lawyers, for instance, rank second highest!).

Barbara Kingsolver reminds us of the worthwhile, good and useful work of farming when she says, "Recall that whatever lofty things you might accomplish today, you will do them only because you first ate something that grew out of dirt."[9] Walking gently includes doing good and satisfying work that makes the world a better place. We strive to have a meaningful life, not just satisfying or meaningful jobs. Many of us are privileged to have much choice in how we spend our hours. May we who have choice exert our privilege wisely and well by choosing meaningful and good work and activity to fill our days.

CONTENTMENT AND BELONGING

Nineteenth-century physician and author Oliver Wendell Holmes said, "I would not give a fig for the simplicity this side of complexity. But I'd give my life for the simplicity on the other side of complexity."[10] Embracing the goodness that has come from progress while also challenging the assumptions of our modern, consumer-driven, technologically enhanced lives moves us toward the other side of complexity. The hope is that we come to a place of contentment, able to remember what matters.

Perhaps finding simplicity on the other side of complexity starts when we name those things that matter to us. Berry identifies justice, ecological well-being, family and community stability, and good work. Simplicity on the other side of complexity comes from evaluating our assumptions about what is important, good, and the ultimate source of human dignity and happiness. What in my lifestyle promotes harmony and what promotes disharmony? How am I thankful? How am I thankless? Do I speak grace through the way I live?

Contentment cannot be experienced in a vacuum: considering only the well-being of my own soul leads to emptiness. Contentment develops over time as we see ourselves as people who belong to God, to others and to the earth from which we come. Walking gently means we are mindful of others, concerned about justice for all, living sustainable lives, guarding and nurturing the earth that supports life. In our desire for a world characterized by *shalom* we "live simply so that others might simply live."[11] As contentment bubbles up from deep within our soul, we are freed from expectations of gaining contentment through owning things or managing to control our circumstances. And so we seek, find and create beauty and good around us, rooting our contentment in things that matter.

QUERIES FOR FURTHER REFLECTION

- Do you live as though the earth belongs to you or as though you belong to the earth? Put another way, do you view the earth as primarily a resource to harness and use or as a gift put under your stewardship to protect, conserve and preserve?

- What technologies do you depend on to enrich your life? What are some implications of your dependency? How has your view of "normal" been affected by various products and pharmaceuticals? (Think of normal aging processes, what a normal body looks like, how a normal body functions or how it should experience feelings.) What effect does your view of "normal" have on your contentment?

- What keeps you from experiencing gratitude to God for good around you? How have you seen gratitude and contentment as being mutually reinforcing in your life?

- "It is not only *our* bodies that have dignity. It is *every* body." What implications could this have for how you live on a day-to-day basis?

- How can you think holistically about living a meaningful life, partnering with God in day-to-day efforts to transform and redeem, rather than just having meaningful work?

- Exercise: Choose one technology or environmental issue to learn more about so you can develop an ethical and informed position. Research both sides, perhaps especially the side you are least inclined to accept.

CRAFTING COMMUNITY

*I swear by my life and my love of it that I will never live for the
sake of another man, nor ask another man to live for mine.*

<small>JOHN GALT IN *ATLAS SHRUGGED*, A NOVEL BY AYN RAND</small>

*Share each other's troubles and problems,
and in this way obey the law of Christ.*

<small>GALATIANS 6:2</small>

Norm Ewert and Sharon Coolidge live simply in an affluent suburb.
They are Wheaton College professors committed to caring for the poor
around the world. Before she and Norm married, Sharon had purchased a
small home a couple blocks from campus. After they married, they expanded and remodeled the 1850s home, using recycled materials (leaded
windows from a school, French doors from a church, a carved staircase
salvaged from a house fire) and adding a reservoir to capture and reuse
rainwater, a solarium with well-placed windows for passive heat, and
thick walls for insulation. As Mennonites they live simply and compas-

sionately, using their resources and energy to help others forge sustainable lives. They are strong supporters of Ten Thousand Villages, a nonprofit program of the Mennonite Central Committee that works with artisans from Third World countries, providing a market and fair prices for their crafts so that they can earn a livable wage. Norm and Sharon extend care toward a broad community, a "home" that reaches far beyond boundaries marked by family, neighborhood, church and nationality. And in caring for others, they find contentment in their own lives.

Some profound moments of contentment come in recognizing that we are part of and belong to something much bigger than ourselves. Conversely, some of our most profound moments of discontent are experienced in isolation, as though we belong to no one or nothing.

To belong to something bigger than ourselves, we must relinquish some measure of control over our circumstances. Sometimes we decide *not to choose* something that we think will bring us contentment, because in choosing it we may harm others or creation. When author and journalist Bill McKibben was a scholar in residence at Middlebury College in Vermont, he wrote: "We're the animal that can decide not to do something we're capable of . . . decide that something else—our family, our tribe, our community, the rest of creation, the divine—matters as much as we do, and thus sets limits on our behavior."[1] When, for the sake of others, people choose not to do something they are capable of doing, they strengthen a sense of responsibility for the well-being of an intangible whole that transcends their individual lives. The world is broken and uncertain, but it is our home.

So we bike, walk or drive a smaller car. We consume less and buy more conscientiously. We choose to turn off the television or isolating video games—or get rid of them altogether. We encourage good citizenship, which is sometimes at odds with a society that depends on good consumers. Instead of following various whims, we choose to stay put in our church and neighborhood, forging strong community ties.

Desiring a sense of community comes naturally enough. Although we are self-determining individuals, we generally yearn to belong. We are social beings with a will to relate, made for relationship, drawn to others.

On a sunny winter afternoon the day following a storm that blanketed us with a foot of snow, I made my way to Herrick Lake for a walk in the woods. I expected to be mostly alone—it was only eighteen degrees outside. But I found that the absence of wind and the presence of sun had drawn a community of like-minded souls with boots, cross-country skis, snowshoes, sleds and ice-fishing paraphernalia. Being alone would have been fine—but finding a community of others who appreciated the beauty and blessing of snow and sun made my soul smile. We greeted each other, knowing that our presence sustained a community of people who have for generations appreciated and celebrated the wonders of a forest wrapped in winter.

We grow wiser and become better people when we invest in the crafting of caring, strong communities in which people sacrifice personal freedoms and conveniences for the sake of children, the elderly, the mentally and physically handicapped, the poor and marginalized. We serve a larger common good when we choose not to consume, develop or build for the sake of preserving the earth's fauna and flora, its natural wonders and resources.

LONGING TO BELONG

Psychology, like technology, deserves two cheers. Both have done humanity good along the way. Psychology uncovered some of the mystery around our human longing to attach at birth, to be held, to belong. But in the pursuit of the good life, some strands of psychology now encourage us to abandon the notion of self-sacrifice as servile. Pop psychology, supported by the philosophy of individualism, has told us to be wary of self-sacrifice or a strong sense of obligation to others because it is detrimental to self-actualization, mental health and thus contentment. We are given permission to pursue whatever beliefs and lifestyle we want, re-gardless of our parents' or our community's values. Truth is relative, and our views about right and wrong are socially constructed. *Free will* and *self-determination* are key words of the day.

Since we are created to attach to others from birth, desiring the giving and receiving nature of relationship and connection, the detachment of the self-determined soul has left us wandering. With no larger body to direct our orbit with a gravitational pull, we have drifted.

Most of us, even if we have a relatively intact desire and ability for at-tachment, will make choices that hurt us and those around us. We try to satisfy longings for connection but sometimes wound others and our-selves in the process. We tend to live by a minimalist ethic that says un-less someone's actions are actually hurting someone else, they ought to be free to choose their own way. They are free to participate or not in the electoral process, to sleep with whomever they want so long as it is con-sensual, to consume unlimited resources so long as they can afford them. A minimalist ethic is an ethic of detachment. It neither strengthens our communities nor brings us contentment.

Sociologist Émile Durkheim studied Western societies in the late nineteenth century. In his classic study on suicide, he found that in so-cieties where rules about how people ought to behave were breaking down, people felt increasingly isolated and anxious. Suicides motivated by this sense of normlessness and disconnection were the result of *anomie*—living in places where expectations of behavior are confused, unclear or absent. Durkheim believed that humans need help regulating egotistical impulses for their own sake, as well as for the health of com-munities. He endorsed a moral liberalism that emphasizes our need for self-discipline and our obligations to others. The capacity to be sacrificial and altruistic is a good and important virtue, he said, and if religion couldn't continue as the guiding light for moral principles, then a civil society would need to rise up and be strong enough to take its place.

RIGHTS AND RESPONSIBILITIES

Singapore has a standard of living that is on par with that of the United States. Women can walk down the street alone at night without fear or anxiety. Singaporeans are free from fears associated with poverty, crime and disorderliness. However, their freedom does not mean being free to pursue personal fulfillment in whatever way an individual defines it. Restrictions on personal freedom in Singapore are stringent. News is owned and censored by the government. Chewing gum is banned, as is eating on the subway or forgetting to flush a public toilet (all of these result in significant fines), and caning is used more than a thousand times a year as public punishment for offenders. Yet there is no unemployment or homelessness, and everyone has medical insurance. Traffic flows without congestion, there is no pollution, and there are plenty of green open spaces.[2]

Whether or not we think Singaporeans are content with this arrangement depends on how we'd load the scales balancing individual freedom and rights on one side, and community obligations and responsibilities on the other. In cultures where contentment and the good life are rooted in community, ties and obligations to others are valued more than individual fulfillment and choice. Freedom means not having to worry about whether or not you (and members of your community) can feed, clothe and shelter your children. The tradeoff is greater restriction of personal choices. Parents focus less on raising children to be independent and more on raising them to be responsible family members and good citizens. Children tend to avoid behaving in ways that might bring shame on their parents, extended family and community. The young marry spouses their parents approve for them, and they live in ways that increase the family's honor and respect. Parents help the young succeed, supporting them as needed, and know that in return they will be cared for and honored in their old age. The young and the old recognize that they belong not to themselves but to the family and community from which they came. Sociologists call such cultures "collectivist" because they emphasize responsibility to group needs over individual rights and aspirations.

In individualistic cultures we define freedom as personal choice—the right to choose our partner, our life path, where we live, what we buy, what kind of work we pursue, who we hang out with, how we express ourselves. We value autonomy, and want acts of good will to be chosen rather than coerced.

Developing a civil society that values responsibility as highly as it does personal rights is the goal of a group of people who call themselves communitarians. They consider communitarianism to be a public philosophy and a social movement made up of academics, writers, politicians, policymakers and ordinary citizens. Communitarians assert that a community can and should develop a shared picture of what it values and what is good, and that a shared vision is preferable to individuals' determining their own values and definitions for what is right or wrong. At the same time, communitarians recognize that communities can be imbalanced and hold wrong beliefs and values. The communitarian movement does not support oppressive marital relationships, for example, but it does support marriages that last, as opposed to liberal divorce laws that make it easier for family ties to be dissolved. Communitarians emphasize the moral obligations people have to families, communities and societies. Rights and responsibilities belong together. Social order and personal liberty are mutually supportive tensions—and communities need to be careful not to overemphasize one or the other.[3] Those of us who value community life are challenged by their principles as we rethink our own claim to personal rights in light of our social and personal responsibilities.

I begin my Sociology of Families course by showing students a quote from Kuwana Haulsey's *The Red Moon*. This novel tells the story of a girl raised in a traditional tribe in Kenya who, at the point of the quote, is trying out the modern ways of her fellow students as she attends a university in Nairobi. She has met a janitor from a tribe similar to her own, and they become friends. At one point he says to her, "Whether you like it or not, it is your family and your tribe that really shapes you. You can fight against that for the rest of your life if you want, but it's much easier to just accept it."[4]

I have my students spend a few minutes journaling a response. Does this quote irk them? Do they agree with the janitor's statement? Whether or not they agree, how do they respond to it as those detaching from family and community back home to attend college and begin an independent life? Those who choose to verbalize their thoughts tend to focus on the need to find their own path, to choose their own way, deviating if necessary from their family or "tribe" even as they recognize the significance of their family's influence on them.

My students, like all of us, are products of the twentieth century, when our greatest obligation became to self-actualize, to be the best we can be, and in that find fulfillment. Self-actualization requires some detachment from our sense of obligation and responsibility to our roots. We are to be loyal primarily to ourselves and make our own bed so long as we are willing to sleep in it.

Alexis de Tocqueville, a French social philosopher, came to the United States in 1831 to see what he could learn about the character of this young democracy. In a two-volume work called *Democracy in America,* he wrote about the "habits of the heart" he observed. A repeated theme that captured his attention was the rugged independence he observed in Americans. He first used the term *individualism* to refer to a kind of state-sanctioned egotism. He admired parts of the American spirit, yet he also saw Americans seeking their opinions only within themselves, becoming increasingly disconnected and unconcerned about society. In his judgment,

individualism, at first, only saps the virtues of public life; but, in
the long run, it attacks and destroys all others [virtues] and is at
length absorbed in downright egotism. . . . They owe nothing to
any man, they expect nothing from any man; they acquire the
habit of always considering themselves as standing alone, and they
are apt to imagine that their whole destiny is in their own hands.
Thus not only does democracy make every man forget his ancestors, but it hides his descendants and separates his contemporaries
from him; it throws him back forever upon himself alone and
threatens in the end to confine him entirely within the solitude of
his own heart.[5]

Tocqueville's critique of the United States is often referred to in arti-
cles and books and used in college courses exploring American politics,
community, religion, and private and civic life. Citizens of the United
States celebrate freedom and equality—strengths Tocqueville identified
in the young democracy. But he warned (and contemporary writers like
Robert Bellah[6] and Robert Putnam[7] affirm) that radical individualism
erodes community ties, diminishing a sense of duty to look out for the
well-being of others. Voting turnout, volunteer work, writing letters to
representatives and newspapers, and involvement in community events
have declined. Care for the elderly, the young, the poor, orphaned and
widowed that was once carried out by families, churches and communities has increasingly come under the responsibility of governmental
agencies.

In our celebration of freedom, we elevated our personal agenda and
rights above obligations to anyone or anything else. Some, like the communitarians, want to help us recognize the cost this exacts on our lives
and the lives of those with whom we live. Instead of freeing us to experience greater happiness, we are overly focused on ourselves, an unhappy and lonely people. Our pursuit of self-fulfillment has not brought

a better world but rather a self-absorbed one.

FORGING STRONG AND CARING COMMUNITIES

Years ago, sometime after the Welcome Wagon had left but before we had scheduled our free haircut or picked up our free pound of premium beef, we became aware of various Wheaton city ordinances. Having moved from the rural U.S. Northwest, we felt a bit overregulated at first. It took awhile to appreciate the need for ordinance sec. 14-27: "removal of dog excrement from property not of owner." Cars couldn't be parked on the street after 2:00 a.m., and community residents were supposed to retrieve garbage and recycling bins from the curb within twenty-four hours of pickup. We quickly learned to take full parenting advantage of the curfew ordinance for minors, and we appreciated ordinances concerning "loud music or noises" and the requirement that businesses remove snow and ice from their sidewalks within twenty-four hours of snowfall. I wondered what story precipitated the ordinance making it unlawful to hunt in the city, but we appreciated that one as well.

Wheaton, like most communities, tries to balance the rights of individuals with public needs for order and safety. So while communities allow drunkenness inside one's home, they do not tolerate drunk driving; parents have the right to discipline their children, but we do not tolerate child abuse; freedom of expression is protected, but vandalism is punished.

Most of us prefer the freedom to choose to do right rather than being forced to do so. We'd rather shovel snow from the sidewalk in front of our home because we are people of good character than because a law requires it. Nor do we want to shovel snow in the fear that if we don't, someone may slip on our property and we will be sued. We prefer the chance to do what is good for the community without being compelled.

Determining what can be left up to people's sense of goodwill and neighborliness and what cannot is tricky business. The more we regulate, the less people choose to do good on their own volition. Weaving between the rights of individuals and the needs of the community is a challenging task.

Some faith-based colleges and universities make their desire to forge strong and caring communities explicit in a written code of conduct that students, and sometimes faculty and staff, sign and are expected to abide by. The following paragraphs come from the preface and introductory comments of the Wheaton College Community Covenant, a statement that all members of the college community are expected to uphold.

[W]hile the College is not a religious order, it yet demonstrates some features that are similar to religious orders, communities wherein, for the sake of fulfilling the community's purposes, its members voluntarily enter into a social compact. At Wheaton we call this social compact our community covenant. . . .

Our mission as an academic community is not merely the transmission of information; it is the development of whole and effective Christians who will impact the church and society worldwide "For Christ and His Kingdom." Along with the privileges and blessings of membership in such a community come responsibilities. The members of the Wheaton College campus community take these responsibilities seriously.

Schools like Wheaton College make an assumption that a community can put obligations on members, even if it means prohibiting personal freedoms that are granted by our larger society. By upholding a covenant they seek to be intentional, voluntary communities driven by a mission that depends on participants' recognizing that privileges of membership come with obligations and opportunities correspond to responsibilities. Sometimes such institutions are caricatured as "total institutions" as described by sociologist Irving Goffman in his exploration of asylums in the 1970s. Total institutions force change on individual behavior by dictating all of life and choreographing all social interactions. Increasing skepticism and decreasing public confidence in the 1960s meant that any institution seeking to shape or channel individual expression or choice became subject to criticism. We valued individual choice and self-determination to the extent that constraints imposed by an institution were likened to the evil "We" denounced by novels such as *Atlas Shrugged* by Ayn Rand.

Alan Ehrenhalt, author of *The Lost City: The Forgotten Virtues of Community in America,* says people do want the good parts of community we idealized from the 1950s, back when Ernie Banks was loyal to the Cubs and neighbors stayed put and knew each other.[8] But a strong sense of community existed in the context of limited choice and a willingness to submit to authority or to the greater good. However much we dislike it, Ehrenhalt asserts that community, limited choice and authority are inextricably linked. Strong communities are forged when people are willing to voluntarily abide by and submit to agreed-upon expectations in spite of any legal right to do otherwise.

DEVELOPING GOOD SAMARITANS

Forging caring communities also requires our willingness to speak up when others' actions are hurtful. I don't like to confront people—I hide behind the idea that it must be someone else's job to quiet noisy teenagers in a movie theater or to remind a hiker tossing aside an empty Fritos bag of the "leave no trace" policy. I'd rather put up with the noise and pick up trash. Yet I appreciate it when someone speaks up in a theater and tells others being disruptive to quiet down. And when my neighbor Joe yelled at a driver to slow down as he sped down our street, I felt a renewed sense that this is my community and I am responsible to speak up for it.

I suppose we all have our threshold, and when I found mine I was thankful to discover I had one. I was watching boys at a local park torment a squirrel by surrounding the small tree it had run to for safety. A couple of the boys tried shaking it free of its life hold on a flimsy branch while others threw rocks at it. I summoned my courage, approached them and told them it was unlawful to torment the park's creatures. (I imagined that somewhere in City Hall there was a town ordinance about this.) They responded with amazing respect and a touch of shame—as though they knew better but had been caught up in a moment of "boys being boys." Perhaps they returned to their squirrel tormenting the next day, but at least for the moment I had replaced anomie with a sense of community responsibility. In the process I accepted my obligation to communicate a vested interest in care of and respect for this public gathering place.

When we confront peers for telling racist or sexist jokes, we are upholding what is good for humanity, embracing people perceived to be "them" as part of "us," whether they live next door or far away and even if they seem more unlike than like us. How big should we draw the circle around the community to which we belong? To whom are we obligated?

When Jesus told a teacher of the law that he must love his neighbor as himself, the teacher asked Jesus, "And who is my neighbor?" (Lk 10:25-37). Jesus then told the story of the Samaritan who acted neighborly to a wounded Jew, who would likely have snubbed and disregarded the Samaritan if he weren't in such desperate straits. Jesus answered the question by saying, "Go and be neighborly." He was unwilling to draw a circle that would leave some outside our responsibility of care.

As Apollo 9 quietly orbited Earth in 1969, astronaut Rusty Schweickart's view of the world was dramatically changing. He started seeing the world as an indivisible whole. Several years later he put into words what he experienced:

Up there you go around every hour and a half, time after time after

time. . . . You wake up over the Mideast, over North Africa . . . and
out over the Indian Ocean . . . and you finally come up across the
coast of California and look for those friendly things: Los Angeles,
and Phoenix, and on across El Paso and there's Houston, there's
home. . . . And you identify with that, you know—it's an attach-
ment. . . . And that identity—that you identify with Houston, and
then you identify with Los Angeles and Phoenix and New Orleans
and everything. And the next thing you recognize in yourself, is
you're identifying with North Africa. You look forward to that, you
anticipate it. And there it is. That whole process begins to shift
what it is you identify with. When you go around it in an hour and
a half you begin to recognize that you identify with the whole
thing. And that makes a change.

You look down there and you can't imagine how many borders
and boundaries you crossed again and again and again. And you
don't even see 'em. At that wake-up scene—the Mideast—you
know there are hundreds of people killing each other over some
imaginary line that you can't see. From where you see it, the thing
is a whole, and it's so beautiful. And you wish you could take one
from each side in hand and say, "Look at it from this perspective.
Look at that. What's important?"[9]

Philosopher Martha Nussbaum argues that we should be world citizens, caring for all humanity. We live in concentric circles: our primary
identity with and obligation toward our family is our innermost circle, but
the circles move outward to include our city, state, nation, and ultimately
we identify with and embrace the world as our global community.

Our political boundaries do have real consequences for how people
live. Economic and political systems vary; we speak different languages
and have different religions, customs and food preferences. We hold dif-
fering ideas about what freedom means and about how to balance the

rights of individuals with public needs for safety and order. But the boundaries are still arbitrary and are drawn and redrawn as history unfolds. As individuals we can choose how broadly we draw the circle around those whom we will embrace.

In one of my classes I use a film called *16 Decisions*. It documents life for the poor in Bangladesh and the good done by a community bank that offers small business loans to women to help better their lives. The documentary follows Salina's life up close. She is a mother as I am, concerned about her children's well-being, belonging to the earth and sharing the same time in history, breathing the same air that I breathe. Our circles of life overlap. Yet she lives so unlike me. Salina has never had a Coke, watched a movie, sat in a recliner, bathed in a tub. She has never used a toaster, a light bulb, a toilet or a sink; her home is a two-room hut made of mud and straw. She cooks outside on fires she keeps going by collecting and burning brush and dung. Salina takes birth control pills that her husband brings home from town to keep her from having more children (the pills cost ten cents for a two-month supply); otherwise she has no contact with medicine or the medical community. The community bank loaned her money so she and her husband could buy a rickshaw that he pedals into town five miles away. On a good day he makes between eighty cents and a dollar providing transportation to those slightly better off than himself. Salina doesn't vote or read, and she met her husband on her wedding day—a marriage arranged by her parents without her consent or consultation.

I don't want to forget her as I drink my mocha, bump up my thermostat on a chilly day, drive my car and buy my groceries. Salina and I belong together in this world; the resources I use to live a comfortable life are as rightfully hers as they are mine. I hold her in my thoughts, praying for her well-being while seeking ways to promote change that would grant her more access to the world's wealth.

Similarly, for a number of years I have held Luis in my prayers. Luis was seven when I "met" him through the 1992 documentary *7 Years Old in America*. I show the video every year—a marvelous film that examines the lives of children from different socioeconomic, racial and regional backgrounds in the United States. At seven Luis was living in a homeless shelter with his mother and two younger siblings; he was a sweet, clever child who had hopes and dreams like any other boy his age. Seven years later the producers interviewed the same children again and released *14 Up in America* in 1998.[10] I had doubted that the producers would be able to find Luis, but they did. At fourteen, he was a resilient youth who had found a church and a faith that helped him stay out of trouble. He had spent four years in foster care between 1992 and 1998; his father had been abusive, and his mother had struggled with drug addictions. By the time he was fourteen, his mother had custody of her children again, and Luis loved and admired how hard she was working to keep the family together. They lived in subsidized housing and used welfare to keep them out of abject poverty. Luis's family will most likely stay poor, yet he remained hopeful that he would rise and realize the American dream.

These must not just be faces on a screen. They are real people, living real lives. In 2006 Luis is out there somewhere, a twenty-two-year-old trying to make his way in the world. Luis and Salina are part of my global village.

That we are American or Bangladeshi, white or black, male or female, rich or poor has significant bearing on how we experience life and relate to others. These different experiences have consequences for justice and *shalom*. Structured inequality is passed down through generations, so that the rich generally stay rich and the poor generally stay poor. Some suburban communities have been built by people who fled urban centers in a white-flight syndrome that separated the haves from the have-nots; they left behind inner cities plagued by low-quality education and inadequate economic opportunities. Some resource-rich countries were colonized by politically powerful ones, and after independence, corporations moved in to capitalize on their resources, maintaining the dependent relationship established during colonization. Again, the poor remain in poverty while the rich grow richer.

Nelson Mandela, former South African president, addressed thousands in Trafalgar Square in February 2005. Speaking of the world community, he said, "Massive poverty and obscene inequality are such terrible scourges of our times . . . that they have to rank alongside slavery and apartheid as social evils." He called for setting free the millions in the world's poorest countries through establishing trade justice, ending rising debts and providing higher-quality aid.[11] In 150 years, will the world look back at us and be amazed at how easily Christians ignored or even justified gross and growing inequality in the world community? Will they look at us the way we look at Christians who supported slavery?

All human beings share a mutual dependence on one ecosystem, one atmosphere in which we were born and on which we all depend. If we are willing, our circle of obligation will extend beyond peoples to creation—to the earth that is our home and will be a home for other generations long after we're gone. If we draw our boundaries large enough to see the earth as our community, then wise use of the world's resources and care for the earth and its creatures is part of our task.

In the grandest vision of a world experiencing *shalom,* we see the poor and the exploited defended and the earth ruled with fairness and truth. Even animals are at peace with each other. Calves and yearlings are safe with lions, and a child can put its hand in a nest of deadly snakes and be unharmed (Is 11:1-9).

As we embrace the whole earth as something to which we belong, we come to love this home of ours—created by God, our temporary dwelling place. We stop thinking of our community and the earth as existing for our personal convenience and well-being and begin to see how we are part of a greater whole. Living in harmony with others and with the created world gives us a foretaste of our yearned-for *shalom*—a vision of a world made right. In work and service, in simple enjoyment of a sunset or a night sky, we come to see that we belong—and in the belonging we work with God to build moral and caring communities that ease our isolation and allow greater contentment to settle in our soul.

TRANSFORMATIVE COMMUNITIES

Bob May died in a work-related accident. Scottie, his wife, is my colleague at Wheaton College and my friend. I knew Bob as a quiet man who preferred listening to talking. At his memorial service, I learned that when extended family gathered, he would dismiss himself from the table to play with his grandchildren rather than sit through after-dinner conversations. I also learned about his strong sense of community and loyalty to his family and his church. He came to family life late, gaining three adolescent children when he married Scottie. He loved them immediately and faithfully. Since he was a self-employed electrician/handyman, he could adapt his schedule to meet needs, such as when he left immediately after a late-night call from a son who, in the prime of the foolishness of youth, needed bailing out of car trouble. On a day's notice Bob drove to New York to help another son install a new boiler—that was a story in itself. He helped widows and single women from church whose houses direly needed the attention he was capable of giving. Story after story was told of how he would hear about a need and immediately see what he could do to meet it. People spoke of how he loved to help others, and they described him as a contented soul. I left the service wanting to be like Bob.

Serving takes us out of our self and places us and our pain in the context of some community. By offering others a good turn as a regular part of our life, we remind ourselves that we are part of something that needs to be nurtured to be strong. Blessing and serving others, such as by volunteering at a soup kitchen or with a program to help teen moms or at-risk youth, strengthens our communities. As we volunteer with an animal shelter or help with fall or spring grounds work at local parks and preserves, we are reminded of the whole to which we belong and from which we draw sustenance. Blessing and serving acknowledge, appreciate and show care for others and creation. They stretch and grow our soul. In serving we receive blessing because we are made for relationship, for community, and to do good. People who socialize with friends and who are involved in church are happier than people who don't. And regardless of how wealthy, educated or diverse a community, those with engaged and active members tend to have less crime, lower mortality and higher academic performance.[12]

In *Whose Keeper? Social Science and Moral Obligation,* Alan Wolfe cautions against assuming that a welfare state like Denmark does much better than a market state like the United States at inspiring individuals to care for the weak and needy. Both allow individuals to be self-focused. In countries with strong welfare systems, the state is given the responsibility to take care of the young, the old, the poor and the handicapped. In market states, people are supposed to be responsible for themselves, and a safety net is supposed to catch the ones who can't or don't. For different reasons, however, in both market states and welfare states, people wash their hands of the responsibility to care for their neighbor or kin.[13] Wolfe challenges readers to recognize that society is a gift that needs to be nurtured by members who accept responsibility to craft moral communities that care for near and distant kin, that recognize a sense of belonging and identity, and invest in the lives of others with whom they share a particular physical space. Bob May modeled this for members of our church and local community. He grew his soul through servanthood.

Sometimes we forget that being social creatures means we have much to gain in the mere act of being social, of giving and taking in relationships. We find contentment, fulfillment and blessing not by consuming or seeking to satisfy our desires but through good citizenship—by engaging, serving and blessing others.

FINDING OUR WAY HOME

In her memoir *Traveling Mercies,* Anne Lamott tells the story of a little girl who got lost one day. Frightened, she ran up and down the streets looking for landmarks that would help her find her way home. Eventually a police officer stopped to help her. They drove around town and at some point came upon the little girl's church. She told him, "You could let me out now. This is my church, and I can always find my way home from there."

Lamott continues: "And that is why I have stayed so close to mine—because no matter how bad I am feeling, how lost or lonely or frightened, when I see the faces of the people at my church, and hear their tawny voices, I can always find my way home."[14]

We have the capacity for relationships that grow deep and wide, sometimes stretching across a lifetime and several generations. Our church families offer us blessing that comes from blended generations of people whose lives are intertwined. They care for us and we for them, and when we lose our way, they help us find our way home to the arms of God.

Sustained communities allow us to be present for the birthing of babies and careers, for the support of the young and aid to each other in loss and hardship. While communities are full of broken people who wound each other, communities offer healing too and hold great potential to lead us into contented lives. Communities are honored when participants recognize that this world we inhabit is far older than we are, will exist long after we do and holds more significance than any of us holds individually. Communities, both local and global, need and deserve our care and respect.

Building communities that move us toward contentment means that we will evaluate and reform them. As community members, we critique and adapt our institutions and traditions to change where they are unjust and to become stronger and more reflective of God's redemptive work in humanity. The Protestant Reformation, the abolition movement, the suffrage movement, Vatican II, the civil rights movement and the environmental movement are examples of efforts to correct errors and assumptions that needed to be challenged and changed.

Of course not all change improves community. Changes that introduced greater choice and individual freedom after the 1960s did as much harm as good to U.S. civic society. The sexual revolution assumed that love is free, a choice without consequences. Women as well as men could sleep with multiple partners without tarnishing their social status. Two people could choose to live together without the convention of marriage to constrain their freedom by imposing obligations. But there were consequences. Sexually transmitted diseases skyrocketed, as did the rate of teenage pregnancy and divorce. Choice and freedom, empty of responsibility, led to increased poverty for women and children, destabilizing family and community life. Today almost 20 percent of children under eighteen in the United States are in poverty, and more than half of those are being raised by single mothers.

Change and reform are necessary for our communities to be strong and to respond to changing demands. We strive to balance private rights with public concerns, wanting to strengthen families, churches, civic society, nation-states and our global village.

One of our struggles with contentment is how to rejoice in our blessings when we see a world we love full of suffering caused by the sins of humanity, including the sins of our own people. Contentment that is neither blind nor naive acknowledges the personal and structural sins of our history and current lives and the need for social justice. We hold a vision of *shalom*, knowing that God will eventually complete the transformative work that has begun. Meanwhile we colabor with God to bring mercy and justice to a world crying out for redemption, and we live simply so others might simply live. We have more wealth to redistribute when we don't live up to or beyond our financial means. We become wise voters and consumers and push for corporate responsibility and accountability worldwide.

Communities that draw us into contentment also embrace the beauty of a world that consistently points to God's glory, persevering and continuing to be reborn spring after spring, generation after generation. Contentment is a braid of three threads—future hope for an earth restored, participation in strengthening present communities and enjoyment of the good that yet abounds around us.

QUERIES FOR FURTHER REFLECTION

- "We're the animal that can decide not to do something we're capable of . . . decide that something else matters as much as we do, and thus sets limits on our behavior." What can you choose *not* to do this week for the sake of something or someone else?

- Where does your sense of community come from? To what communities do you feel most connected? How can you invest in, foster and enrich a connection this week?

- Is Singaporeans' life worth the personal rights they give up for it? What from your cultural heritage inclines you to put your rights ahead of your obligations? How might meeting some obligation you have draw you toward greater contentment?

- Is there a Salina (*16 Decisions*) or a Luis (*7 Years Old in America*) you could pray for, someone whose story you could be mindful of as you walk through a rather privileged life at the same time they walk through theirs?

- Is your contentment primarily a passive rejoicing in the good you have? What are you doing, and what can you do to make a greater contribution to *shalom* in the world?

- Exercise: Look for a way to be a good Samaritan this week—go out of your way to do someone some good. Afterward, reflect on the impact it had on your soul, on your sense of contentment and of belonging to a community outside yourself.

REMEMBERING

So in the room called Remember it is possible to find peace—the peace that comes from looking back and remembering to remember that though most of the time we failed to see it, we were never really alone.

FREDERICK BUECHNER

Juncos are sitting in a snow-dusted tree outside my window. They come *south to Chicago* every winter, to escape the cold of Canada! I look forward to them—the charcoal-gray males and soft brown females with dark eyes and tail feathers that flash a white V as they flit from branch to branch. I suppose I am seeing the very same birds return to this spot every year, and I marvel that they remember the way.

Creation remembers the tasks of each season. Salmon find their way back to their birthplace to spawn; spiders instinctively know how to spin webs. As my spot on the earth tilts nearer the sun, birds return north, daffodils bloom, and the grass greens up almost overnight. The cut tulips I bring inside stretch toward the sun by late afternoon, thirsting for the light and warmth that called them forth. I like to think of these acts of nature as holy remembrances. The earth groans, longing for redemption, we are told in Romans 8, yet the earth and its creatures remember how to wake from dormancy, to bud, bloom, grow, reproduce, spin, burrow, build hives and nests, fly and sing.

Humanity has a different mechanism for remembering. We are less gifted with instinct and more dependent on each generation's passing down the language, stories, knowledge, skills and songs of prior generations. Memory is a collective task. Collective memory holds our experiences together, so that we are not disconnected souls living without connection to our past or our future. Jews observe the Passover, remembering how God rescued them from slavery under the Egyptians. Christians observe Easter and the Eucharist to remember the death and resurrection of Jesus, who gives us life. In our observances we remember that God is ever present and we were never, are never, alone.

In an essay for *Books & Culture,* Peter Chattaway writes, "Few themes in the Bible are as persistent as the call to remember."[1] His essay is a film critique that considers how memory has become a movie theme in such films as *Memento, The Bourne Identity* and *The Bourne Supremacy,* and *Eternal Sunshine of the Spotless Mind.* Chattaway notes that these movies often deal with redemption, a wiping clean of the slate so one can start again, yet also with atonement, retrieving one's memory to make right the wrongs of the past. In all these films there is a struggle to remember who one is, what matters and what mistakes have been made that need to be set right.

Peace comes, Frederick Buechner says, from remembering that we are not alone.[2] Contentment is rooted in the work and love of God. The incarnation, death and resurrection of Jesus set in motion God's redemptive plan for creation and made it possible for us to be fully reconciled to God. Jesus, the exemplar of God's love, shows us how to live well, and God's Spirit empowers us to follow his example. We can walk lightly, contentment strengthening our step, because God will never forsake us. God calls us by name to remember who we are and what has been done for us, to remember what matters and to learn from our mistakes.

REMEMBERING WHO WE ARE

Macrina Wiederkehr has found our name. She found it as she explored the meaning of her own name. She asked someone who knew Greek to help her figure out what Macrina means, and the best he could come up with was "Little-Great-One." And so we all are, she says: Little-Great-Ones. Her last name means "return again." Little-Great-One Come Home. Wiederkehr finds an identity in her name that helps her remember who she is:

> All too often we bemoan our imperfections rather than embrace them as part of the process in which we are brought to God. Cherished emptiness gives God space in which to work. We are pure capacity for God. Let us not, then, take our littleness lightly. It is a wonderful grace. It is a gift to receive. At the same time, let us not get trapped in the confines of our littleness, but keep pushing on to claim our greatness. Remind yourself often, I am pure capacity for God; I can be *more*.[3]

Recognizing that we are both great and small helps us remember who we are. Some of us think too highly of ourselves, others too little, and most of us think too much about ourselves—whether too highly or too little. We remember who we are as we remember our history and the people from whom we've come.

In collectivist cultures, people tend to remember their lineage. Family lines are tracked carefully, and ancestors are honored. Family members know their history, the mistakes, the acts of courage, the hardships endured, the achievements accomplished. They learn from and draw courage and comfort from their family story. A lot of us can't remember much further back than our grandparents, and even their life stories seem mostly unknown or irrelevant to us. Even while our memory of stories may be weak, though, many families have someone who is tracking the family genealogy—at least the names, birth and death dates, marriages and children. We know that who we are is connected to and shaped by the people of our past.

When my mother came to Illinois for her surgery, staying with each of her daughters for a week at a time, we all got to know each other in ways we hadn't before. Mark saw how much I am like my mother—how we use similar mannerisms, tending to articulate only partial ideas or mix up our thoughts and words, yet still understand each other. When we are together, I often ask about her family stories, wanting to know her more and perhaps better understand who I am through her stories.

This time we talked about Aunt Ruth, who died in her early forties of multiple sclerosis. Aunt Ruth left the family church—the German Congregational Church—and joined the Catholic Church right after high school. I asked what Grandma and Grandpa and her brothers and sisters thought of it all, and Mom told me the story. Ruth became disenchanted with Christianity after learning that the pastor of their church "took advantage" of one of her classmates (perhaps they had sex—Mom was unclear on this point). Grandpa and the rest of the siblings stopped going to church after that. But Grandma kept taking Mom, who was too young to understand the scandal anyway. Aunt Ruth reclaimed her faith when she found a Christianity she could trust in the Catholic-run nursing school she attended after high school. Uncle Art, the family's diplomat and big brother, pleaded with her not to become a nun, because it would devastate their parents. And so Aunt Ruth, who had not yet taken her vows, left the convent. Shortly after that she married Uncle Johnny, and they raised my cousins in the Catholic Church.

I thought on that story for quite some time—especially on how each generation since has had some who felt compelled to redefine the Christianity of her or his family, to find God and faith in places unexplored by siblings and parents. My own differences with my father over matters of conviction were a source of tension in our relationship for too many years. I loved God deeply, yet my father struggled to imagine how I could refuse to submit to a patriarchal structure he believed was ordained by God. And I think of one of our daughters, who would say that after spending a couple of years searching and reflecting, she retains most of the beliefs of her childhood faith. Even though her beliefs differ from mine at some points, I am satisfied that we are close enough. I think Dad ultimately felt the same about me, and I wonder if Grandma did about Aunt Ruth.

I experience peace in recognizing that God has been present and faithful all these years. The concerns of one generation are similar to those of our parents and grandparents, and we learn from remembering the stories that make up our histories. We find peace as we recognize, whether or not we knew it, that we were never alone.

REMEMBERING WHAT MATTERS

The Grand Story is about God, who created a good universe. God gave humans choice, knowing they would choose badly and that their choices would affect the whole earth. But from the beginning God set a plan in motion to send Jesus to show us how to live well, to atone for our rebellion and to bring about the redemption of creation, giving witness to God's love.

It's a simple story—creation, fall, redemption—and we echo this epic in smaller stories told in our sonnets, plays, novels and histories. Faithful God sustains, carries and works through frail human beings to bring about redemption. And that matters. We come from God, belong to God and are invited to participate in God's redemptive plan. As we remember, we enter a shared identity with all creation. Abbot Basil Pennington says:

> By the intuition of the Spirit we come to know our solidarity with
> all being. This cannot but lead to compassion—compassion for

our fellow humans who are one with us in our Source, in our call, and in our fate. We will know that in their completeness lies our completeness, and vice versa. . . . Moreover, we will know that oneness and compassion with the rest of creation that is the source of good stewardship and a true ecology.[4]

Contentment is rooted in remembering. Life is not about my happiness but about the joy of recognizing that we all emerge from one source—and that source is God who loves us, redeems us and calls us to share in the task of bringing peace, justice and healing to creation.

REMEMBERING OUR MISTAKES

We remember Pearl Harbor, 9/11 and Hurricane Katrina. We remember the stock market crash of 1929, Woodstock and walking on the moon in 1969. We "remember the Alamo." But how much of history do we remember accurately? And how much of history is distorted so that we look more virtuous, braver and stronger than we really were? For authentic contentment to come from remembering, we need the courage to look accurately at our history and remember our mistakes—both personal mistakes and collective ones.

The Alamo represents something quite different to Mexicans, whose ancestors were fighting to defend their land and way of life, from what it represents to Anglo Texans. Columbus Day is a day of grief among indigenous people, who lived free lives before Christopher Columbus came and claimed the Americas for Spain. Columbus's diaries and letters record that he expected to find wealth that belonged to others and to seize it for himself and his sponsors. The year following his "discovery" of America (the Caribbean islands) in 1492, he returned with a second expedition of seventeen ships that came to invade and conquer. Columbus instituted slavery and systematic extermination of the Taíno people inhabiting the islands, and his success led the way for other Europeans to arrive and lay claim to land already occupied by others.[5]

Do we remember our history accurately? Does our memory allow us to acknowledge and repent of our sins?

We are predisposed to have a distorted memory of wrongs others have done us personally as well and tend to recall less accurately the wrongs we have done to others. In our disagreements with colleagues, friends, parents, siblings, spouses or children, most of us view ourselves as more innocent and the other as more guilty. We harbor bitterness rather than seek forgiveness, and contentment eludes us. We need to remember our mistakes, to note our sins, to repent. Feelings of contentment that have not involved our looking at our sin and seeking repentance for it are shallow and ultimately unsatisfying.

In Chattaway's essay he says: "Augustine recognized that his own memory was flawed, and so he ultimately appealed to the memory of the transcendent God, who alone has a perfect view of reality, and can thus keep our 'scattered selves' united to each other and to him." This requires a fair amount of humility—a recognition that our memories are flawed and a willingness to be taught, to have the gaps in our knowledge filled in, to think about restitution as part of righting wrongs.

A gift of my father's cancer was that we had time to reconcile before he died. It gave us time to think about our relationship. He asked me at one point if there was anything between us, anything left that we needed to address, to forgive. But by that time we had both named our sins, forgiven and extended forgiveness. By that time we had remembered who we were—children loved by God. Contentment born of humility recognizes that we belong to God and to each other, allowing us to confront our sins, to learn from our mistakes and to remember who we are.

GOD'S FAITHFULNESS

Israel was a people that remembered. In addition to remembering and celebrating God's rescuing them from Egypt with the Passover, the Jews celebrated the Festival of Booths as a yearly reminder of the forty years between their release from bondage in Egypt and their finding a permanent homeland. During the festival they built and lived in temporary shelters for eight days, reminding them of this life's temporal nature and of their dependence on God.

God commanded Israel to remember, so altars were built to commemorate particular moments when God stepped in and saved them from their troubles. The people wore amulets on their foreheads for memory, and they would assemble to hear a recounting of their history and of God's faithfulness. David remembers God's faithfulness in his psalms, even as he cries out in present danger or pain. Today Jews still assemble for the High Holy Days to remember God's wonderful deeds for their ancestors.

The biblical narrative gives us a picture of a people loved, blessed and remembered by God. The memory of the biblical Jews lapsed at times; ours does too, and we turn toward evil gain, forgetting the God of our salvation. Yet God faithfully woos us back—sometimes through hardship, in Israel's case often through subjugation by other nations that lasted for generations. God stays faithful and present, ever giving our hearts the opportunity to turn back to God's loving embrace.

Contented souls remember. Remembering turns our mind to what matters, and it requires effort, because the needs of the day demand attention and energy that drain our capacity to remember. The Christian practice of Holy Communion, "Do this in remembrance of me," calls our faith communities to gather and remember together the life, death and resurrection of Jesus. We remember that we have been forgiven, reconciled and welcomed into the loving embrace of God. We are, after all, "okay" because of God's atoning work. Contented souls remember that they belong to God, not to themselves, and that they are part of a life stream that includes all of creation, stretching back to the beginning and forward into the future long after they're gone. Finally, we remember that ultimate happiness is not found in external circumstances but in a trust that we are made for eternity. God is present now, yet we are souls that will one day be brought into the direct presence of the God who created and loves us.

CHOOSING JOY

Chale, the dog who had been my companion for twelve years, died during the writing of this book. I knew she was nearing her end, given the slowness with which she was rising to greet me, still willing and seemingly eager for our walks but slower to climb the steps up and down the porch. She took several days to die, wanting to burrow into bushes or sleep in the sun. I'd sit with her some and leave her alone some, and at night, because she had not yet died, carried her back inside. The next morning Mark and I carried her out near the back fence, placing her and her bed where the warmth of the fall sunshine could reach her. I sat with her some, and she died when I left her for a while. I wonder now if she preferred not to die in my presence, knowing the grief her leaving would bring me. But in her dying I witnessed a peaceful acceptance of the suffering that comes from living.

The world is characterized more by paradox than by opposites. Light mutes to gray, and while we tend to equate "darkness" with "evil," darkness also brings cool night air on hot summer nights, rightly slows down the activity of humans and allows us to see the stars and the craters of the moon. Joy and suffering are also paradoxical. Suffering allows us to identify with Christ's suffering, and it helps us identify with the magnitude of suffering that exists all around us. In suffering we finally experience the sufficiency of God's grace once all other options have been exhausted, and we learn to look to God as the ultimate source of *shalom* and rest. We bear witness to God's faithfulness in the joy that eases our suffering and the promise that this temporal life is only our beginning. The paradox, the mystery, of contentment found in the midst of struggle

and hardship is important to name and carry with us. We bring contentment into the uncertainty of our present by remembering the goodness
of God's faithfulness as it stretches back through all past generations,
eras and eons.

Choosing to live joyfully requires some measure of fortitude. Henri
Nouwen reminds us of this in *The Return of the Prodigal Son:*

> This is a real discipline. It requires choosing for the light even
> when there is much darkness to frighten me, choosing for life even
> when the forces of death are so visible, and choosing for the truth
> even when I am surrounded with lies. I am tempted to be so im-
> pressed by the obvious sadness of the human condition that I no
> longer claim the joy manifesting itself in many small but very real
> ways. The reward of choosing joy is joy itself. There is so much re-
> jection, pain, and woundedness among us, but once you choose to
> claim the joy hidden in the midst of all suffering, life becomes cele-
> bration. Joy never denies the sadness, but transforms it to a fertile
> soil for more joy.
>
> People who have come to know the joy of God do not deny the
> darkness, but they choose not to live in it. They claim that the light
> that shines in the darkness can be trusted more than the darkness
> itself and that a little bit of light can dispel a lot of darkness. They
> point each other to flashes of light here and there, and remind each
> other that they reveal the hidden but real presence of God. They
> discover that there are people who heal each other's wounds, for-
> give each other's offenses, share their possessions, foster the spirit
> of community, celebrate the gifts they have received, and live in
> constant anticipation of the full manifestation of God's glory.[6]

Pronouncing words has an effect on us. When I say, "I choose joy. I
am content," I begin to create a willingness and desire to pursue contentment in spite of my circumstances. We can live in anticipation of God's

glory by deriving pleasure in moment-by-moment observation of the beauty and wonder of this life, this earth. A delicate drop of water on a rose petal, a well-acted play, frogs singing, the smell of bread, climbing Multnomah Falls, a choir anthem, Mark's hands rubbing my shoulders. There is so much beauty and goodness. When I am gone, I will miss this marvelous earth that is my home.

I don't know what heaven holds. I hope the picture is close to the one C. S. Lewis paints in *The Last Battle,* the final book in his well-loved Narnia series. Lewis envisions a perfect replication of earth (or in this case, Narnia), unimaginably greener, clearer, more fragrant, more alive, richer in sound and touch. What a glorious heaven that would be!

I have found much to love here, in spite of the suffering, the pain and the disappointment. Yet a world with only beauty awaits us. But before we get there, at the end of *this* day, may we have found much beauty amidst the ashes of our human existence. May our souls be satisfied because of how we have lived with others. May we have learned to sip and savor the good gifts of this most beautiful, amazing earth. And may we enter heaven's rest having lived a contented life, walking each day in remembrance of the God who remembers us.

QUERIES FOR FURTHER REFLECTION

- Contentment is rooted in remembering. What stories from your family demonstrate the faithfulness of God and help you remember the strength, fortitude and blessing that have always come alongside the heartache and struggle of your family's history?

- Which of your stories might you be recalling in ways that make you look better than you really did? Of what sins do you need to repent? Who have you wounded? With whom do you need to reconcile? What bitterness do you harbor that keeps you from forgiving and seeking forgiveness? Are you attempting to find a kind of contentment that would allow you to avoid confronting your own sin?

- Exercise: Contentment requires remembering that we belong to God and others and are part of creation, that we have been forgiven and reconciled to God, and that our ultimate happiness is not found in external circumstances but in God's faithfulness and presence. Meditate on these thoughts, and then write down and say out loud every day: "I choose joy; I choose contentment." Pronounce these words; let them lay claim to your soul.

NOTES

Chapter 1: An Invitation to Contentment

[1]Daniel L. Migliore, *Faith Seeking Understanding: An Introduction to Christian Theology* (Grand Rapids, Mich.: Eerdmans, 2004), pp. 190-91.

[2]C. W. Mills, *The Sociological Imagination* (London: Oxford University Press, 1959).

[3]C. S. Lewis, *Mere Christianity* (New York: Collier/Macmillan, 1943), p. 36.

Chapter 2: Seeing the Self as Soul

[1]Dallas Willard, *Renovation of the Heart: Putting on the Character of Christ* (Colorado Springs, Colo.: NavPress, 2002), p. 37.

[2]Jeffrey H. Boyd, *Reclaiming the Soul: The Search for Meaning in a Self-Centered Culture* (Cleveland: Pilgrim's, 1996).

[3]See Jonathan Hill's brief history of the Enlightenment in the IVP Histories series, *Faith in the Age of Reason* (Downers Grove, Ill.: InterVarsity Press, 2004), for an accessible discussion covering Galileo to Kant.

[4]Thorstein Veblen, an American economist, first coined the term in *The Theory of the Leisure Class: An Economic Study of Institutions* (New York: Macmillan, 1902). It was picked up and popularized in the 1960s.

[5]Marc Gobe and Sergio Zyman, *Emotional Branding: The New Paradigm for Connecting Brands to People* (New York: Watson-Guptill, 2001).

[6]Alina Wheeler, *Designing Brand Identity: A Complete Guide to Creating, Building, and Maintaining Strong Brands* (Somerset, N.J.: Wiley, 2003).

[7]Tess Rheinhardt, "Clarity of Mind in Media and Culture 0," *Adbusters* 13, no. 11 (January/February 2005).

[8]Joel Bakan, *The Corporation: The Pathological Pursuit of Profit and Power* (New York: Free Press, 2004).

[9]Ibid., p. 121.

[10]Ibid., p. 122.

[11]Thomas Merton, *No Man Is an Island* (New York: Harcourt Brace, 1955), p. 230.

[12]Maya Angelou, *I Know Why the Caged Bird Sings* (New York: Random House, 1970), p. 26.

Chapter 3: The Practice of Fortitude

[1]Jean-Pierre de Caussade, *The Sacrament of the Present Moment* (San Francisco: Harper & Row, 1982), p. 64.

[2]Daniel L. Migliore, *Faith Seeking Understanding: An Introduction to Christian Theology* (Grand Rapids, Mich.: Eerdmans, 2004), p. 133.

[3]Francis Fukuyama, *Our Posthuman Future: Consequences of the Biotechnology Revolution* (New York: Farrar, Straus and Giroux, 2002), p. 46.

[4]Barry Yeoman, "Less Sleep, More Energy," *Reader's Digest,* October 2004, pp. 103-8.

[5]See Leonore Tiefer, *Sex Is Not a Natural Act* (Jackson, Tenn.: Westview, 2004), and Tracy Gaudet, *Consciously Female* (New York: Bantam, 2004), for excellent discussions of the medicalization of sexuality.

[6]Jeffrey P. Hantover, "The Boy Scouts and the Validation of Masculinity," in *Men's Lives,* ed. Michael S. Kimmel and Michael A. Messner, 3rd ed. (Boston: Allyn and Bacon, 1995), p. 77.

[7]John Bly, *Iron John* (New York: Addison-Wesley, 1990).

[8]There are multiple types of men's movements. Men's rights, fathers' rights, gay rights, a profeminist movement—all these are contemporary men's movements. Bly propelled a movement forward, but there is no singular Men's Movement.

[9]John Eldredge, *Wild at Heart: Discovering the Secret of a Man's Soul* (Nashville: Thomas Nelson, 2001).

[10]However, spouse and child abuse rates suggest many people live *private* lives that are very unsafe, dangerous and difficult.

[11]Albert Borgmann, *Power Failure: Christianity in the Culture of Technology* (Grand Rapids, Mich.: Brazos, 2003), and Hantover, "Validation of Masculinity," p. 77.

Chapter 4: Mellowness of Heart

[1]The authorship of this poem has long been a mystery. Niebuhr himself supposedly denied writing it and attributed it to Friedrich Oetinger, an eighteenth-century theologian. However, Niebuhr's widow claims that Niebuhr himself wrote it. She preferred the shorter version, but I offer it here in its entirety as it was originally written. See <http://en.wikiquote.org/wiki/Reinhold_Niebuhr>.

[2]David M. Newman, *Sociology of Families* (Thousand Oaks, Calif.: Pine Forge, 1999), p. 58.

[3]Albert Borgmann, *Power Failure: Christianity in the Culture of Technology* (Grand Rapids, Mich.: Brazos, 2003).

[4]Ellen Charry, "On Happiness," *Anglican Theological Review* 86, no. 1 (Winter 2004): 19-33.

[5]Ronald Rolheiser, *The Holy Longing: The Search for Christian Spirituality* (New York: Doubleday, 1999).

[6]Richard Foster, *Freedom of Simplicity: Finding Harmony in a Complex World* (New York: HarperPaperbacks, 1981), p. 120.

[7]Robert A. Heinlein, *Stranger in a Strange Land* (New York: Ace, 1961), pp. 387-88.

[8]C. S. Lewis., *Perelandra* (New York: Macmillan, 1944), pp. 68-69.

[9]Jeremiah Burroughs, *The Rare Jewel of Christian Contentment* (1648; reprint, Carlisle, Penn.: Banner of Truth Trust, 1964), p. 228.

[10]D. G. Tendulkar, *Mahatma,* 2nd ed. (Ahmedabad, India: Navajivan, 1960), 2:278.

[11]Gordon Bass, "On Safety Patrol," Everyday Heroes, *Reader's Digest,* June 2005, pp. 27-30.

[12]Lynn Rosellini, "The Whistle-Blower," Everyday Heroes, *Reader's Digest,* February 2005, pp. 25-28.

[13]Andrea Cooper, "Full House," *Reader's Digest,* April 2005, pp. 95-101.

[14]Joni Eareckson Tada, *The God I Love: A Lifetime of Walking with Jesus* (Grand Rapids, Mich.: Zondervan, 2003).

[15]A. J. Conyers, "Can Postmodernism Be Used as a Template for Christian Theology?" *Christian Scholar's Review* 33, no. 3 (Spring 2004): 293.

Chapter 5: Embracing Limits

[1]I want to thank my anthropologist colleague Dean Arnold for helping clarify this for me.

[2]Janet Kornblum, "Aging Face: Love It or Lift It?" *USA Today*, May 24, 2004, p. 6D.

[3]See Wendell Berry's essay "Why I'm Not Going to Buy a Computer," in *What Are People For?* (New York: Northpoint, 1990), pp. 170-77.

[4]Roger Olson, "Where Community Is No Cliché," *Christianity Today*, February 2005, pp. 56-61. Also see the group's webpage at <www.homesteadheritage.com>.

[5]Ellis Jones, Ross Haenfler, Brett Johnson and Brian Klocke, *The Better World Handbook: From Good Intentions to Everyday Actions* (Gabriola Island, B.C.: New Society, 2001).

[6]Ronald Rolheiser, *The Holy Longing: The Search for Christian Spirituality* (New York: Doubleday, 1999).

[7]I checked this out with biologist Fred Van Dyke, who directs the Environmental Studies program at Wheaton College. He also said, "We all know that if we get enough scholars together someone will disagree with something, however obvious."

Chapter 6: Sipping and Savoring

[1]Wayne Muller, *Sabbath: Finding Rest, Renewal and Delight in Our Busy Lives* (New York: Bantam, 1999), p. 49.

[2]Thich Nhat Hanh, *Living Buddha, Living Christ* (New York: Riverhead, 1995), p. 3.

[3]Linda Breen Pierce, *Choosing Simplicity: Real People Finding Peace and Fulfillment in a Complex World* (Carmel, Calif.: Gallagher, 2000).

[4]As quoted by Mark Greer, "Strengthen Your Brain by Resting It," *Monitor on Psychology* 35 (July/August 2004): 60.

[5]Such as Cheryl Spinweber, Scripps Mercy Sleep Disorders Center; Richard Bootzin, University of Arizona; Tracy Kuo, Stanford Sleep Disorders Clinic; James Maas, Cornell University; and David Dinges, University of Pennsylvania School of Medicine.

[6]See its website for further information: <www.slowfood.com>.

[7]A lot of information about free-range meat is available on the Internet. A good beginning place is <www.freerangegraphics.com/flash/flash3.html>; click on the movie clip called "The Meatrix." Following the clip are multiple links to a variety of helpful sites.

[8]Check out <www.groundhog.org>, which is the official site of the Punxsutawney groundhog club.

[9]Muller, *Sabbath*, p. 45.

[10]Lynne M. Baab, *Sabbath Keeping: Finding Freedom in the Rhythms of Rest* (Downers Grove, Ill.: InterVarsity Press, 2005).

Chapter 7: Walking Gently

[1]N. Katherine Hayles, *How We Became Posthuman: Virtual Bodies in Cybernetics, Literature and Informatics* (Chicago: University of Chicago Press, 1999), p. 3.

[2]The United Nations and Amnesty International both have informative websites explaining

conflict diamonds and what is being done and can be done—including the ways consumers purchase diamonds. See <www.un.org/peace/africa/Diamond.html> or <www.amnestyusa.org> for starters.

[3]The video and book *The Corporation: The Pathological Pursuit of Profit and Power* by Joel Bakan (New York: Free Press, 2004) offer a compelling look at corporations and suggest ways we can begin to hold them accountable.

[4]Ellis Jones, Ross Haenfler, Brett Johnson and Brian Klocke, *The Better World Handbook* (Gabriola Island, B.C.: New Society, 2001).

[5]Go to <www.earthday.net/footprint/index.asp> to take this quiz for yourself.

[6]Bakan, *Corporation*, p. 72.

[7]See the Interface website: <www.interfacesustainability.com/whatis.html>.

[8]From the *General Social Surveys 1972-2000: Cumulative Codebook* (Chicago: National Opinion Research Center, 2001), pp. 1391-1409.

[9]Barbara Kingsolver, quoted in *The Essential Agrarian Reader: The Future of Culture, Community and the Land,* ed. Norman Wirzba (Lexington: University Press of Kentucky, 2003).

[10]Oliver Wendell Holmes, quoted in *Simplicity and Success: A Newsletter About Creating What Matters Most in Life and Work* 1, no. 4 (February 15, 2003): 1.

[11]While this axiom has widespread use, Mahatma Gandhi was the first to have said it: "Live simply so others might simply live."

Chapter 8: Crafting Community

[1]Bill McKibben, "The Environment: Part 1, Restraint," *Adbusters* 13, no. 1 (January/February 2005).

[2]David G. Myers, *The American Paradox: Spiritual Hunger in an Age of Plenty* (New Haven, Conn.: Yale University Press, 2000), p. 178.

[3]Amitai Etzioni, Andrew Volmert and Elanit Rothschild, *The Communitarian Reader: Beyond the Essentials* (New York: Rowman & Littlefield, 2004), p. 13.

[4]Kuwana Haulsey, *The Red Moon* (New York: Ballantine, 2001), p. 224.

[5]Alexis de Tocqueville, *Democracy in America* (New York: Walker, 1847), 2:585-86.

[6]Robert Bellah et al., *Habits of the Heart: Individualism and Commitment in American Life* (Berkeley: University of California Press, 1985).

[7]Robert D. Putnam, *Bowling Alone: The Collapse and Revival of American Community* (Riverside, N.J.: Simon & Schuster, 2001).

[8]Alan Ehrenhalt, *The Lost City: The Forgotten Virtues of Community in America* (New York: Basic Books, 1995).

[9]As quoted in Peter M. Senge, *The Fifth Discipline: The Art and Practice of the Learning Organization* (New York: Doubleday Currency, 1990), pp. 369-70.

[10]The producers plan to follow the children every seven years until they are twenty-eight years old, following the English study that has documented the lives of the same children in Great Britain every seven years starting in 1963 with *7 Up*. The most recent installment, *42 Up*, was released in 1999.

[11]See <www.cnn.com/2005/WORLD/europe/02/03/Mandela.london/index.html>.

[12]Myers, *American Paradox*, pp. 181-82.

[13]Alan Wolfe, *Whose Keeper? Social Science and Moral Obligation* (Los Angeles: University of California Press, 1989).

[14]Anne Lamott, *Traveling Mercies: Some Thoughts on Faith* (New York: Anchor, 1999), p. 55.

Chapter 9: Remembering

[1]Peter T. Chattaway, "Forget Me Not," *Books & Culture,* January/February 2005, p. 14.

[2]Frederick Buechner, *A Room Called Remember* (New York: HarperSanFrancisco, 1992), p. 8.

[3]Macrina Wiederkehr, *A Tree Full of Angels: Seeing the Holy in the Ordinary* (New York: Harper & Row, 1988), p. 27.

[4]M. Basil Pennington, in *Living with Apocalypse*, ed. Tilden H. Edwards (New York: HarperCollins, 1984), quoted in *A Guide to Prayer for All God's People,* ed. Rueben P. Job and Norman Shawchuck (Nashville: Upper Room, 1990), p. 126.

[5]Ward Churchill, *Indians Are Us* (Monroe, Maine: Common Courage, 1994).

[6]Henri Nouwen, *The Return of the Prodigal Son* (New York: Image, 1994), p. 117.

Name Index

Subject Index

How to Contact the Author

Visit Lisa Graham McMinn's website at www.lisamcminn.com. There you'll find more information about her books and speaking schedule. Her most current contact information is there as well.